COOKIES

recipes for gifting & sharing

MADE WITH Love

pil

Publications International, Ltd.

Pictured on the front cover: Frosted Butter Cookies *(page 150)*, Gingerbread People *(page 170)* and Chocolate Reindeer *(page 154)*.

Pictured on the back cover *(left to right, top to bottom):* Black and White Sandwich Cookies *(page 72)*, White Chocolate Peppermint Brownies *(page 102)*, Refrigerator Cookies *(page 32)*, Cashew-Lemon Shortbread *(page 24)*, Festive Candy Canes *(page 147)*, Gooey Thumbprints *(page 57)*, Flourless Peanut Butter Cookies *(page 28)* and Rum Fruitcake Cookies *(page 156)*.

Photographs on front cover and pages 1, 4, 5, 6, 7, 151 and 172 copyright ©Shutterstock.com.

ISBN: 978-1-68022-541-9

Library of Congress Control Number: 2016941649

Manufactured in China.

8 7 6 5 4 3 2 1

Microwave Cooking: Microwave ovens vary in wattage. Use the cooking times as guidelines and check for doneness before adding more time.

CONTENTS

THE PERFECT PRESENT 4

CLASSICS FOR CHRISTMAS 10

CHOCOLATE DECADENCE 35

FESTIVE FRUIT FAVORITES 56

ELEGANT NIBBLES 70

YULETIDE BARS AND BROWNIES 95

INTERNATIONAL CHEER 118

SANTA'S FAVORITE COOKIES 146

GIFTS FROM A JAR 172

INDEX 188

THE PERFECT PRESENT

Homemade cookies always make wonderful gifts. Of course they're standard at the holidays, but they also make great gifts any time of the year: Mother's Day, Father's Day, Valentine's Day, birthdays, housewarming gifts, thank-you gifts and party favors.

MAKING ENOUGH

Before you shop for ingredients, plan how many cookie gifts you will need and how many cookies will be included in each gift. Decide how many cookies each gift will contain (for example, 12 for an individual, 24 for a family and 40 for a workplace) and calculate how many cookies you will need. If you need more cookies than a single recipe yields, make separate batches of dough instead of doubling the recipe.

If you're planning on giving elaborately decorated cookies like Frosted Butter Cookies (page 150), consider also including one or two simple high-yield cookies like White-Chocolate-Macadamia Nut Cookies (page 18), Gooey Thumbprints (page 57) or Chocolate-Dipped Cinnamon Thins (page 160). You'll still have a fabulously impressive cookie gift but in a fraction of the time.

When you're making a lot of cookies, plan on one day for making dough and one day for baking (and maybe even another day for decorating). Most cookie dough can be made ahead and refrigerated for a day or two; in fact, some dough requires it and in many cases this improves the flavor of the finished cookie. Wrap the dough tightly in plastic wrap, and label it if you're making more than one type.

DECORATING

Many cookies can be made extra special with a few simple decorating techniques.

• **Cookie glaze.** Sift 1 cup of powdered sugar into a small bowl. Stir in milk, cream or citrus juice by teaspoonfuls until the glaze reaches drizzling consistency. Drizzle the glaze over your cookies with a small spoon or fork and then sprinkle with decorating sugars. Let the cookies stand until the glaze is set.

• **Chocolate dipped.** Melt high-quality bittersweet chocolate (60 percent cacao) in a small saucepan over low heat until melted, stirring constantly. Transfer the chocolate to a small deep bowl. Dip each cookie halfway into the chocolate, scraping the bottoms on the edge of the bowl to remove excess chocolate, then place the cookies on a waxed paper-lined baking sheet.

Sprinkle with multicolored sprinkles or decors and let the cookies stand at room temperature or refrigerate until the chocolate is set. Try this with Triple Chipper Monsters (page 12), Refrigerator Cookies (page 32), Black and White Sandwich Cookies (page 72) or Chocolate Strawberry Stackers (page 78).

PACKAGING

When you're giving several different kinds of cookies, be aware that cookies packaged together will affect each other's flavors; subtly flavored cookies like butter cookies or shortbread will pick up stronger flavors like coffee, chocolate or gingerbread. If you're planning on packing all the cookies in one box or basket, wrap the cookies with the strong flavor separately in a cellophane bag before boxing them.

TYPES OF PACKAGES

Keep an eye out all year for interesting packaging and, if you have storage space, stock up on containers during post-holiday sales. Craft supply stores and online retailers are excellent resources for cookie packaging.

• **Tins and boxes.** These work well for fragile cookies, or cookies that will be shipped. Look for bakery boxes at craft supply stores or online, or reuse solid decorative gift boxes. Pack cookies in cellophane bags or line the container with tissue paper, decorative dish towel or cloth napkin before loosely packing with cookies.

• **Cellophane bags.** Clear bags are available in various shapes and sizes, ranging from small enough for individual cookies to large enough to hold an entire batch of cookies. Close the bags with the included twist-ties and then secure with ribbon. Add a decorative label, or place in a gift bag.

• **Vintage china plates or bowls, glass cake plates, cookie jars or brightly colored baking dishes.** Vintage shops, flea markets and garage sales are great sources for quirky and unique containers for cookies. Arrange cookies on the dish or platter, then tightly wrap with clear clingy plastic wrap or cellophane and tie with a bow.

• **Trays.** Party supply stores sell a variety of disposable and reusable trays in colors, patterns and metallic finishes. Trays are perfect for large cookie displays at parties or offices.

GIFT IDEAS

• **Study Gift for the Student.** Package Holiday Biscotti (page 152) or Apricot Biscotti (page 66) in wide-mouth half-gallon canning jars, glass canister jars or cellophane bags and include coffee, tea or hot chocolate mix.

• **Ultimate Holiday Cookie Tray.** Holiday Triple Chocolate Yule Logs (page 168), Chocolate Raspberry Thumbprints (page 64), Gingerbread People (page 170), Chocolate Cherry Cookies (page 68), Browned Butter Spritz Cookies (page 164) and Rum Fruitcake Cookies (page 156). Arrange the cookies on a vintage holiday tray, on a disposable plastic tray or in a large hat box.

• **Housewarming Gift.** Make bar cookies in a new 13×9-inch baking pan (see pages 94–117). Cool completely and cut into squares, then wrap the whole pan with cellophane and tie with a bow. Or make Chocolate Chip Sour Cream Brownies (page 96) in a new decorative ceramic baking dish and include an oven mitt and a spatula.

• **Wedding or Baby Shower Party Favors.** Wrap single cookies or pairs of cookies in small cellophane bags and tie with color-coordinated ribbon. Cut Chocolate Reindeer (page 154) or Frosted Butter Cookies (page 150) into wedding bell, umbrella or footprint shapes, or letters in the happy couple's or baby's initials.

CLASSICS FOR CHRISTMAS

PEANUT BLOSSOMS

Makes about 4 dozen cookies

¼ cup sugar
1 package (about 15 ounces) yellow cake mix
1 cup peanut butter
⅓ cup butter, softened
1 egg
50 milk chocolate kiss candies, unwrapped

1. Preheat oven to 350°F. Line cookie sheets with parchment paper. Place sugar in small bowl.

2. Beat cake mix, peanut butter, butter and egg in large bowl with electric mixer at medium speed until well blended.

3. Shape dough into 1-inch balls; roll in sugar. Place 2 inches apart on prepared cookie sheets. Press one candy into center of each ball, flattening dough slightly.

4. Bake 10 minutes or until lightly browned. Cool on cookie sheets 2 minutes. Remove to wire racks; cool completely.

BASIC OATMEAL COOKIES

Makes 3 dozen cookies

2 cups old-fashioned oats

1⅓ cups all-purpose flour

¾ teaspoon baking soda

½ teaspoon baking powder

½ teaspoon salt

1 cup packed brown sugar

¾ cup (1½ sticks) butter, softened

¼ cup granulated sugar

1 egg

1 tablespoon honey

1 teaspoon vanilla

1. Preheat oven to 350°F. Line cookie sheets with parchment paper.

2. Combine oats, flour, baking soda, baking powder and salt in medium bowl.

3. Beat brown sugar, butter and granulated sugar in large bowl with electric mixer at medium speed until light and fluffy. Add egg, honey and vanilla; beat until well blended. Gradually add flour mixture about ½ cup at a time; beat at low speed just until blended. Drop dough by tablespoonfuls about 2 inches apart onto prepared cookie sheets.

4. Bake 11 to 15 minutes or until cookies are puffed and golden. *Do not overbake.* Cool on cookie sheets 5 minutes. Remove to wire racks; cool completely.

BUTTERSCOTCH-COCONUT OATMEAL COOKIES: Prepare Basic Oatmeal Cookies with the following variations. Decrease oats to ¾ cup and brown sugar to ½ cup. Melt ½ cup butterscotch chips and add to sugar mixture with egg. Stir ½ cup flaked coconut and ½ cup chopped pecans into dough with flour mixture.

TRIPLE CHIPPER MONSTERS

Makes about 2 dozen cookies

2½ cups all-purpose flour

1 teaspoon baking soda

¾ teaspoon salt

1 cup (2 sticks) butter, softened

1 cup packed brown sugar

½ cup granulated sugar

2 eggs

2 teaspoons vanilla

2 cups semisweet chocolate chips

½ cup white chocolate chips

½ cup butterscotch or peanut butter chips

1. Preheat oven to 350°F. Line cookie sheets with parchment paper.

2. Combine flour, baking soda and salt in medium bowl.

3. Beat butter, brown sugar and granulated sugar in large bowl of electric mixer at medium speed until light and fluffy. Beat in eggs and vanilla until blended. Gradually beat in flour mixture at low speed until well blended. Stir in chips. Drop dough by scant ¼ cupfuls 3 inches apart onto prepared cookie sheets. Lightly flatten dough with fingertips.

4. Bake 12 to 14 minutes or until edges are set and golden brown. Cool cookies on cookie sheets 2 minutes. Remove to wire racks; cool completely.

LEMON MELTS

Makes about 3½ dozen cookies

2 cups all-purpose flour

½ teaspoon cream of tartar

½ teaspoon baking soda

½ cup powdered sugar

½ cup packed brown sugar

½ cup canola oil

½ cup (1 stick) butter, melted

1 tablespoon lemon juice

1 tablespoon vanilla

1½ teaspoons almond extract

1. Preheat oven to 350°F. Line cookie sheets with parchment paper.

2. Combine flour, cream of tartar and baking soda in medium bowl.

3. Beat powdered sugar, brown sugar, oil, butter, lemon juice, vanilla and almond extract in large bowl with electric mixer at medium speed until smooth. Gradually beat in flour mixture until stiff dough forms. Drop dough by rounded tablespoonfuls 2 inches apart onto prepared cookie sheets; flatten slightly with fork.

4. Bake 20 minutes or until edges are lightly browned. Cool on cookie sheets 1 minute. Remove to wire racks; cool completely.

SNICKERDOODLES

Makes about 2 dozen cookies

¾ cup plus 2 tablespoons sugar, divided

2 teaspoons ground cinnamon, divided

1⅓ cups all-purpose flour

1 teaspoon cream of tartar

½ teaspoon baking soda

½ teaspoon salt

½ cup (1 stick) butter, softened

1 egg

1. Preheat oven to 375°F. Line cookie sheets with parchment paper. Combine 2 tablespoons sugar and 1 teaspoon cinnamon in small bowl.

2. Combine flour, remaining 1 teaspoon cinnamon, cream of tartar, baking soda and salt in medium bowl.

3. Beat remaining ¾ cup sugar and butter in large bowl with electric mixer at medium speed until creamy. Beat in egg. Gradually add flour mixture, beating at low speed until stiff dough forms. Roll dough into 1-inch balls; roll in cinnamon-sugar mixture. Place on prepared cookie sheets.

4. Bake 10 minutes or until set. *Do not overbake.* Remove to wire racks; cool completely.

WHITE CHOCOLATE MACADAMIA NUT COOKIES

Makes about 3 dozen cookies

1½ cups all-purpose flour

½ teaspoon salt

¼ teaspoon baking soda

1½ cups packed brown sugar

⅔ cup shortening

2 eggs

1 teaspoon vanilla

1 cup white chocolate chips

1 cup macadamia nuts, coarsely chopped

1. Preheat oven to 375°F.

2. Combine flour, salt and baking soda in medium bowl.

3. Beat brown sugar and shortening in large bowl with electric mixer at medium-high speed until light and fluffy. Add eggs, one at a time, beating well after each addition. Beat in vanilla. Add flour mixture; beat at low speed just until blended. Stir in white chocolate chips and nuts. Drop dough by rounded tablespoonfuls 2 inches apart onto ungreased cookie sheets.

4. Bake 9 to 11 minutes or until cookies are set. Cool on cookie sheet 2 minutes. Remove to wire racks; cool completely.

CLASSIC CHOCOLATE CHIP COOKIES

Makes about 2 dozen cookies

1¼ cups all-purpose flour

½ teaspoon salt

½ teaspoon baking soda

½ cup (1 stick) butter, softened

½ cup granulated sugar

¼ cup packed brown sugar

1 egg

1 teaspoon vanilla

1 cup semisweet chocolate chips

Coarse salt or sea salt flakes

1. Preheat oven to 350°F. Line cookie sheets with parchment paper.

2. Combine flour, ½ teaspoon salt and baking soda in medium bowl.

3. Beat butter, granulated sugar and brown sugar in large bowl with electric mixer at medium speed until light and fluffy. Add egg and vanilla; beat until well blended. Add flour mixture; beat just until blended. Stir in chocolate chips. Drop tablespoonfuls of dough 2 inches apart onto prepared cookie sheets. Sprinkle tops with coarse salt.

4. Bake 10 to 12 minutes or until edges are lightly browned. Cool on cookie sheets 1 minute. Remove to wire racks; cool completely.

BUTTER PECAN CRISPS

Makes about 6 dozen cookies

2½ cups sifted all-purpose flour

1 teaspoon baking soda

1 cup (2 sticks) butter, softened

¾ cup granulated sugar

¾ cup packed brown sugar

½ teaspoon salt

2 eggs

1 teaspoon vanilla

1½ cups finely ground pecans

30 pecan halves

4 ounces semisweet chocolate

1 tablespoon shortening

1. Preheat oven to 375°F. Line cookie sheets with parchment paper.

2. Combine flour and baking soda in small bowl.

3. Beat butter, granulated sugar, brown sugar and salt in large bowl with electric mixer at medium speed until light and fluffy. Add eggs, one at a time, beating well after each addition. Beat in vanilla and ground pecans. Gradually stir in flour mixture.

4. Spoon dough into large pastry bag fitted with ⅜-inch round tip; fill bag halfway. Shake down dough to remove air bubbles. Hold bag perpendicular to, and about ½ inch above, prepared cookie sheets. Pipe dough into 1¼-inch balls, spacing 3 inches apart. Cut each pecan half lengthwise into 2 slivers. Press 1 sliver in center of each dough ball.

5. Bake 10 minutes or until lightly browned. Cool on cookie sheets 5 minutes. Remove to wire racks; cool completely.

6. Melt chocolate and shortening in small heavy saucepan over low heat, stirring constantly until melted and smooth. Drizzle over cookies. Let stand until set.

CASHEW–LEMON SHORTBREAD COOKIES

Makes about 2½ dozen cookies

½ cup roasted cashew nuts

1 cup (2 sticks) butter, softened

½ cup plus 2 tablespoons sugar, divided

2 teaspoons lemon extract

1 teaspoon vanilla

2½ cups all-purpose flour

1. Preheat oven to 325°F.

2. Place cashews in food processor; process until finely ground. Add butter, ½ cup sugar, lemon extract and vanilla; process until well blended. Add flour; pulse until dough begins to form a ball.

3. Shape dough into 1½-inch balls; roll in remaining 2 tablespoons sugar. Place 2 inches apart on ungreased cookie sheets; flatten slightly.

4. Bake 17 to 19 minutes or just until set. Remove to wire racks; cool completely.

NEW ENGLAND RAISIN SPICE COOKIES

Makes about 5 dozen cookies

2¼ cups all-purpose flour

2 teaspoons baking soda

1 teaspoon salt

¾ teaspoon ground cinnamon

¼ teaspoon ground ginger

¼ teaspoon ground cloves

⅛ teaspoon ground allspice

1½ cups raisins

1 cup packed brown sugar

½ cup shortening

¼ cup (½ stick) butter

1 egg

⅓ cup molasses

Granulated sugar

1. Combine flour, baking soda, salt, cinnamon, ginger, cloves and allspice in medium bowl. Stir in raisins.

2. Beat brown sugar, shortening and butter in large bowl with electric mixer at medium speed until creamy. Add egg and molasses; beat until fluffy. Gradually add flour mixture, stirring until just blended. Cover; refrigerate at least 2 hours.

3. Preheat oven to 350°F. Shape heaping tablespoons of dough into balls. Roll in granulated sugar. Place 2 inches apart on ungreased cookie sheets.

4. Bake 8 minutes or until golden brown. Cool on cookie sheets 1 minute. Remove to wire racks; cool completely. Store in airtight container.

FLOURLESS PEANUT BUTTER COOKIES

Makes 2 dozen cookies

1 cup packed brown sugar

1 cup creamy peanut butter

1 egg, lightly beaten

½ cup semisweet chocolate chips, melted

1. Preheat oven to 350°F. Beat brown sugar, peanut butter and egg in medium bowl until blended and smooth.

2. Shape dough into 24 (1½-inch) balls. Place 2 inches apart on ungreased cookie sheets. Flatten dough slightly with fork.

3. Bake 10 to 12 minutes or until set. Remove to wire racks; cool completely. Drizzle with chocolate.

VARIATION: Press a milk chocolate star or milk chocolate kiss candy into each cookie ball before baking instead of drizzling with melted chocolate.

BLACK AND WHITE HEARTS

Makes about 3½ dozen cookies

1 cup (2 sticks) butter, softened

¾ cup sugar

3 ounces cream cheese, softened

1 egg

1½ teaspoons vanilla

3 cups all-purpose flour

1 cup semisweet chocolate chips

2 tablespoons shortening

1. Beat butter, sugar, cream cheese, egg and vanilla in large bowl with electric mixer at medium speed until light and fluffy. Add flour; beat until well blended. Divide dough in half; wrap each half in plastic wrap. Refrigerate 2 hours or until firm.

2. Preheat oven to 375°F. Roll dough to ⅛-inch thickness on lightly floured surface. Cut dough with lightly floured 2-inch heart-shaped cookie cutter. Place cutouts 1 inch apart on ungreased cookie sheets. Bake 7 to 10 minutes or until edges are lightly browned. Immediately remove to wire racks; cool completely.

3. Melt chocolate chips and shortening in small saucepan over low heat, stirring constantly until smooth. Dip half of each heart into melted chocolate. Refrigerate on cookie sheets or trays lined with waxed paper until chocolate is set. Store covered in refrigerator.

REFRIGERATOR COOKIES

Makes about 4 dozen cookies

1¾ cups all-purpose
   flour
¼ teaspoon baking
   soda
¼ teaspoon salt
½ cup granulated
   sugar
¼ cup light corn syrup
¼ cup (½ stick) butter,
   softened
2 eggs
1 teaspoon vanilla
   Decors, sprinkles
   and colored sugars

1. Combine flour, baking soda and salt in medium bowl.

2. Beat granulated sugar, corn syrup and butter in large bowl with electric mixer at medium speed. Add eggs and vanilla; beat until well blended. Stir in flour mixture at low speed just until blended.

3. Shape dough into two logs 1½ inches in diameter. Wrap in plastic wrap. Freeze 1 hour.

4. Preheat oven to 350°F. Line cookie sheets with parchment paper. Cut dough into ¼-inch-thick slices; place 1 inch apart on prepared cookie sheets. Sprinkle with colored sugar, if desired.

5. Bake 8 to 10 minutes or until edges are golden brown. Remove to wire racks; cool completely.

VARIATIONS: For citrus cookies, stir 1 teaspoon grated orange peel into butter mixture. For chocolate chip cookies, stir ½ cup mini chocolate chips into dough with flour mixture. For chocolate cookies, stir 2 tablespoons unsweetened cocoa powder into flour mixture. For sugar-rimmed cookies, roll logs in colored sugar before slicing.

CHOCOLATE DECADENCE

CLASSIC BROWNIES

Makes 2 dozen brownies

1 cup all-purpose flour

½ cup unsweetened cocoa powder

½ teaspoon salt

½ teaspoon baking powder

½ cup (1 stick) butter, softened

2 ounces cream cheese

1 cup sugar

2 eggs

1 teaspoon vanilla

½ cup semisweet chocolate chips (optional)

1. Preheat oven to 350°F. Spray 9-inch square baking pan with nonstick cooking spray. Combine flour, cocoa, salt and baking powder in small bowl.

2. Beat butter and cream cheese in large bowl with electric mixer at high speed until smooth. Add sugar, eggs and vanilla; beat until smooth. Add flour mixture; mix at low speed just until blended. Spread batter in prepared pan.

3. Bake 15 to 20 minutes or until toothpick inserted into center comes out clean. Sprinkle with chocolate chips, if desired; cool completely in pan. Cut into squares or rectangles.

CHOCOLATE MARSHMALLOW DROPS

Makes about 3 dozen cookies

1¾ cups all-purpose flour

⅓ cup unsweetened cocoa powder

1 teaspoon baking soda

½ teaspoon salt

1 cup sugar

½ cup (1 stick) butter

¼ cup milk

1 egg

1 teaspoon vanilla

16 to 18 large marshmallows, cut into halves

Chocolate Glaze (recipe follows)

36 pecan halves (optional)

1. Preheat oven to 350°F. Combine flour, cocoa, baking soda and salt in small bowl.

2. Beat sugar and butter in large bowl with electric mixer at medium speed until light and fluffy. Add milk, egg and vanilla; beat until well blended. Gradually add flour mixture, beating until blended. Drop dough by rounded teaspoonfuls onto ungreased cookie sheets.

3. Bake 8 minutes. Remove from oven; gently press 1 marshmallow half, cut side down, onto each cookie. Return to oven 3 to 4 minutes or until marshmallows are softened and cookies are set. Cool on cookie sheets 1 minute. Remove to wire racks; cool completely.

4. Prepare Chocolate Glaze; drizzle over cookies. Top with pecans, if desired.

CHOCOLATE GLAZE: Combine ⅓ cup whipping cream and 1 tablespoon butter in small saucepan; bring to a boil over high heat. Place ½ cup semisweet chocolate chips in medium bowl. Pour cream mixture over chocolate; let stand 5 minutes. Stir until smooth.

MALTED MILK COOKIES

Makes about 4 dozen cookies

1 cup (2 sticks) butter, softened

¾ cup granulated sugar

¾ cup packed brown sugar

1 teaspoon baking soda

2 eggs

2 ounces unsweetened chocolate, melted and cooled to room temperature

1 teaspoon vanilla

2¼ cups all-purpose flour

½ cup malted milk powder

1 cup chopped malted milk balls

1. Preheat oven to 375°F.

2. Beat butter in large bowl with electric mixer at medium speed until creamy. Add granulated sugar, brown sugar and baking soda; beat until blended. Add eggs, chocolate and vanilla; beat until well blended. Beat in flour and malted milk powder until blended. Stir in malted milk balls. Drop dough by rounded tablespoonfuls 2 inches apart onto ungreased cookie sheets.

3. Bake about 10 minutes or until edges are set. Cool on cookie sheets 1 minute. Remove to wire racks; cool completely.

MOCHA BROWNIE COOKIES

Makes 5 to 6 dozen cookies

2½ cups all-purpose flour

⅓ cup unsweetened cocoa powder

1 teaspoon baking soda

1 teaspoon baking powder

1 teaspoon salt

1 cup granulated sugar

¾ cup packed brown sugar

½ cup (1 stick) butter, softened

¼ cup sour cream

1 tablespoon instant coffee, dissolved in 2 tablespoons hot water

2 eggs

1½ cups semisweet chocolate chips

1. Preheat oven to 325°F. Combine flour, cocoa, baking soda, baking powder and salt in medium bowl.

2. Beat granulated sugar, brown sugar, butter, sour cream and coffee mixture in large bowl with electric mixer at medium speed until creamy. Add eggs, one at a time, beating well after each addition until batter is light and fluffy.

3. Gradually add flour mixture to butter mixture, beating at low speed until just blended. Beat at medium speed 1 minute or until well blended. Stir in chocolate chips. Drop dough by rounded tablespoonfuls onto ungreased cookie sheets.

4. Bake 9 to 11 minutes or until slight imprint remains when pressed with finger. Cool on cookie sheets 3 minutes. Remove to wire racks; cool completely.

DARK CHOCOLATE DREAMS

Makes 10 to 12 cookies

½ cup all-purpose flour

¾ teaspoon ground cinnamon

½ teaspoon baking powder

¼ teaspoon salt

16 ounces bittersweet chocolate, coarsely chopped

¼ cup (½ stick) butter

1½ cups sugar

3 eggs

1 teaspoon vanilla

1 package (12 ounces) white chocolate chips

1 cup chopped pecans, lightly toasted*

*To toast pecans, spread in single layer on ungreased baking sheet. Bake in preheated 350°F oven 5 to 7 minutes or until light brown, stirring occasionally

1. Preheat oven to 350°F. Line cookie sheets with parchment paper. Combine flour, cinnamon, baking powder and salt in small bowl.

2. Combine chocolate and butter in large microwavable bowl. Microwave on HIGH 2 minutes; stir. Microwave 1 to 2 minutes, stirring after 1 minute, or until chocolate is melted. Cool slightly.

3. Beat sugar, eggs and vanilla with electric mixer at medium-high speed about 6 minutes or until very thick and pale. Reduce speed to low; gradually beat in chocolate mixture until well blended. Gradually beat in flour mixture until blended. Fold in white chocolate chips and pecans.

4. Drop dough by level ⅓ cupfuls 3 inches apart onto prepared cookie sheets. Flatten dough into 4-inch circles with fingers covered in plastic wrap.

5. Bake 12 minutes or just until firm and surface begins to crack. *Do not overbake.* Cool cookies on cookie sheets 2 minutes. Remove to wire racks; cool completely.

SURPRISE COOKIES

Makes 1 dozen cookies

2 ounces semisweet baking chocolate, coarsely chopped

1¼ cups all-purpose flour

½ teaspoon baking powder

¼ teaspoon salt

½ cup (1 stick) butter, softened

½ cup sugar

1 egg

1 teaspoon vanilla

Fillings: drained maraschino cherries or candied cherries; white chocolate chunks; chocolate chunks; raspberry jam or apricot preserves

Sprinkles or nonpareils (optional)

1. Preheat oven to 350°F. Spray 12 mini (1¾-inch) muffin cups with nonstick cooking spray.

2. Melt semisweet chocolate in small heavy saucepan over low heat, stirring constantly; remove from heat. Combine flour, baking powder and salt in small bowl.

3. Beat butter and sugar in large bowl with electric mixer at medium speed 2 minutes or until light and fluffy. Beat in egg and vanilla. Beat in melted chocolate. Gradually add flour mixture, beating at low speed until blended.

4. Drop dough by level teaspoonfuls into prepared muffin cups. Form small indentation in centers; fill with desired fillings. Top with heaping teaspoonful of dough, smoothing top lightly. Top with sprinkles, if desired.

5. Bake 15 to 17 minutes or until set. Cool completely in pan.

CHOCOLATE COCONUT TOFFEE DELIGHTS

Makes 1 dozen large cookies

½ cup all-purpose flour

¼ teaspoon baking powder

¼ teaspoon salt

1 package (12 ounces) semisweet chocolate chips, divided

¼ cup (½ stick) butter, cut into small pieces

¾ cup packed brown sugar

2 eggs, beaten

1 teaspoon vanilla

1½ cups flaked coconut

1 cup toffee baking bits

½ cup dark chocolate chips

1 teaspoon shortening

1. Preheat oven to 350°F. Line cookie sheets with parchment paper. Combine flour, baking powder and salt in small bowl.

2. Place 1 cup semisweet chocolate chips and butter in large microwavable bowl. Microwave on HIGH 1 minute; stir. Microwave at additional 30-second intervals, stirring after each interval until mixture is melted and smooth.

3. Beat brown sugar, eggs and vanilla in large bowl with electric mixer at medium speed. Beat in chocolate mixture until well blended. Add flour mixture; beat at low speed until blended. Stir in coconut, toffee bits and remaining 1 cup semisweet chocolate chips. Drop dough by heaping ⅓ cupfuls 3 inches apart onto prepared cookie sheets. Flatten with rubber spatula into 3½-inch circles.

4. Bake 15 to 17 minutes or until edges are firm to the touch. Cool on cookie sheets 2 minutes; slide parchment paper and cookies onto wire racks. Cool completely.

5. For chocolate drizzle, melt dark chocolate chips and shortening in small microwavable bowl on HIGH 1 minutes; stir. Microwave at additional 30-second intervals until smooth. Drizzle over cookies using fork. Let stand until set.

CHUNKY DOUBLE CHOCOLATE COOKIES

Makes about 3 dozen cookies

4 ounces unsweetened chocolate, chopped

2 cups all-purpose flour

1½ teaspoons baking powder

½ teaspoon salt

1½ cups packed brown sugar

¾ cup (1½ sticks) butter, softened

1 teaspoon vanilla

2 eggs

12 ounces white chocolate, chopped

1 cup chopped nuts (optional)

1. Preheat oven to 350°F. Melt unsweetened chocolate in small saucepan over low heat, stirring constantly. Cool slightly.

2. Combine flour, baking powder and salt in medium bowl.

3. Beat brown sugar, butter and vanilla in large bowl with electric mixer at medium speed until light and fluffy. Add eggs; beat until well blended. Beat in melted chocolate. Gradually add flour mixture, beating well at low speed after each addition. Stir in white chocolate and nuts, if desired. Drop by rounded tablespoonfuls 2 inches apart onto ungreased cookie sheets.

4. Bake 11 to 12 minutes or until set. Cool on cookie sheets 1 minute. Remove to wire racks; cool completely. Store in airtight container up to 1 week.

DEEP DARK CHOCOLATE DROPS

Makes about 3 dozen cookies

1¼ cups all-purpose flour

¼ cup unsweetened cocoa powder

½ teaspoon baking soda

½ teaspoon salt

1½ cups semisweet chocolate chips, divided

½ cup (1 stick) butter, softened

½ cup granulated sugar

¼ cup packed brown sugar

1 egg

2 tablespoons milk

1 teaspoon vanilla

1. Preheat oven to 350°F. Line cookie sheets with parchment paper. Combine flour, cocoa, baking soda and salt in medium bowl.

2. Place ½ cup chocolate chips in small microwavable bowl. Microwave on HIGH 1 minute; stir. Microwave at additional 30-second intervals, stirring after each interval, until melted and smooth. Cool slightly.

3. Beat butter, granulated sugar and brown sugar in large bowl with electric mixer at medium speed until light and fluffy. Add egg, milk, vanilla and melted chocolate; beat until well blended. Add flour mixture; beat just until blended. Stir in remaining 1 cup chocolate chips. Drop dough by rounded tablespoonfuls 2 inches apart onto prepared cookie sheets.

4. Bake 10 minutes or until set. Cool on cookie sheets 2 minutes. Remove to wire racks; cool completely.

MOCHA DOTS

Makes 6 dozen cookies

1 tablespoon instant coffee granules

2 tablespoons hot water

1½ cups all-purpose flour

¼ cup unsweetened cocoa powder

½ teaspoon baking soda

½ teaspoon salt

½ cup (1 stick) butter, softened

½ cup granulated sugar

¼ cup packed brown sugar

1 egg

1 teaspoon vanilla

72 chocolate nonpareil candies (about 1 inch in diameter)

1. Preheat oven to 350°F. Line cookie sheets with parchment paper. Dissolve instant coffee granules in hot water; cool slightly. Combine flour, cocoa, baking soda and salt in medium bowl.

2. Beat butter, granulated sugar and brown sugar in large bowl with electric mixer at medium speed until light and fluffy. Add egg, coffee mixture and vanilla; beat until well blended. Add flour mixture; beat until well blended.

3. Shape level teaspoonfuls of dough into balls; place 2 inches apart on prepared cookie sheets. Gently press 1 candy onto center of each ball. (Do not press candies too far into dough balls. Cookies will spread around candies as they bake.)

4. Bake 7 to 8 minutes or until set and no longer shiny. Cool on cookie sheets 2 minutes. Remove to wire racks; cool completely.

EXTRA-CHOCOLATEY BROWNIE COOKIES

Makes 3 dozen cookies

2 cups all-purpose flour

½ cup unsweetened Dutch process cocoa powder

1 teaspoon baking soda

¾ teaspoon salt

1 cup (2 sticks) butter, softened

1 cup packed brown sugar

½ cup granulated sugar

2 eggs

2 teaspoons vanilla

1 package (11 ounces) semisweet chocolate chunks

2 cups coarsely chopped walnuts or pecans

1. Preheat oven to 350°F. Whisk flour, cocoa, baking soda and salt in medium bowl until well blended.

2. Beat butter in large bowl with electric mixer at medium speed 1 minute or until light and fluffy. Add brown sugar and granulated sugar; beat 2 minutes or until fluffy. Add eggs and vanilla; beat until well blended. Add flour mixture; beat at low speed until blended. Stir in chocolate chunks and walnuts.

3. Drop dough by heaping tablespoonfuls 2 inches apart onto ungreased cookie sheets; flatten slightly.

4. Bake 8 to 10 minutes or until set. Cool on cookie sheets 2 minutes. Remove to wire racks; cool completely. Store in airtight container at room temperature up to 4 days.

FESTIVE FRUIT FAVORITES

GOOEY THUMBPRINTS

Makes about 3 dozen cookies

1 cup (2 sticks) butter, softened

½ cup powdered sugar

2 tablespoons packed brown sugar

¼ teaspoon salt

1 egg

2 cups all-purpose flour

¼ cup strawberry, grape or apricot jam or chocolate-hazelnut spread

1. Beat butter, powdered sugar, brown sugar and salt in large bowl with electric mixer at medium speed 2 minutes or until light and fluffy. Add egg; beat until well blended. Add flour, ½ cup at a time, beating well at low speed after each addition.

2. Shape dough into disc; wrap tightly in plastic wrap. Refrigerate at least 1 hour or until firm.

3. Prepare and chill cookie dough as directed. Preheat oven to 300°F.

4. Shape dough into 1-inch balls; place 1 inch apart on ungreased cookie sheets. Make small indentation in each ball with thumb; fill with heaping ¼ teaspoon jam.

5. Bake 25 to 27 minutes or until tops of cookies are light golden brown. Cool on cookie sheets 1 minute. Remove to wire racks; cool completely.

AUTUMN APPLE BARS

Makes about 3 dozen bars

1 package (15 ounces) refrigerated pie crusts (2 crusts)

1 cup graham cracker crumbs

8 tart cooking apples, peeled and sliced ¼ inch thick (8 cups)

1 cup plus 2 tablespoons granulated sugar, divided

2½ teaspoons ground cinnamon, divided

¼ teaspoon ground nutmeg

1 egg white

1 cup powdered sugar

1 to 2 tablespoons milk

½ teaspoon vanilla

1. Preheat oven to 350°F. Roll out one pie crust to 15×10-inch rectangle on lightly floured surface. Place on bottom of ungreased 15×10-inch jelly-roll pan.

2. Sprinkle graham cracker crumbs over dough; layer apple slices over crumbs. Combine 1 cup granulated sugar, 1½ teaspoons cinnamon and nutmeg in small bowl; sprinkle over apples.

3. Roll out remaining pie crust to 15×10-inch rectangle; place over apple layer. Beat egg white in small bowl until foamy; brush over top crust. Stir remaining 2 tablespoons granulated sugar and remaining 1 teaspoon cinnamon in separate small bowl; sprinkle over crust. Bake 45 minutes or until lightly browned.

4. Combine powdered sugar, 1 tablespoon milk and vanilla in small bowl. Add additional milk, if necessary, to reach desired consistency. Drizzle over top. Cut into bars.

COCOA-ORANGE-CRANBERRY BARS

Makes 12 to 16 bars

½ cup dried cranberries

2 tablespoons thawed frozen orange juice concentrate

1 cup sugar

½ cup unsweetened cocoa powder

½ cup (1 stick) butter, melted

2 eggs

2 teaspoons grated orange peel

2 teaspoons vanilla

¾ cup all-purpose flour

½ teaspoon baking powder

¼ teaspoon salt

½ cup white chocolate chips

½ cup chopped pecans

1. Preheat oven to 350°F. Grease 9-inch square baking pan.

2. Combine cranberries and orange juice concentrate in medium microwavable bowl. Microwave on HIGH 30 seconds. Cover and let stand 5 minutes.

3. Beat sugar, cocoa and butter in medium bowl until well blended. Add eggs, orange peel and vanilla; beat until well blended. Stir in flour, baking powder and salt just until blended. Stir in cranberry mixture. Spread batter in prepared pan. Sprinkle evenly with chocolate chips and pecans.

4. Bake 30 minutes or until toothpick inserted into center comes out clean. Cool completely in pan on wire rack. Cut into squares.

APPLE BUTTER COOKIES WITH PENUCHE FROSTING

Makes about 4¹/₂ dozen cookies

1 cup (2 sticks) butter, softened

½ cup granulated sugar

½ cup packed brown sugar

1 cup unsweetened apple butter

1 egg

1 teaspoon vanilla

2 cups all-purpose flour

1 teaspoon baking powder

1 teaspoon baking soda

1 teaspoon ground cinnamon

¼ teaspoon salt

¾ cup chopped toasted walnuts* or raisins

Penuche Frosting (page 63)

*To toast walnuts, spread in single layer on ungreased baking sheet. Bake in preheated 350°F oven 5 to 7 minutes or until lightly browned, stirring occasionally.

1. Preheat oven to 350°F. Line cookie sheets with parchment paper.

2. Beat butter, granulated sugar and brown sugar with electric mixer on medium speed until creamy. Add apple butter, egg and vanilla; beat until light and fluffy. Gradually add flour, baking powder, baking soda, cinnamon and salt, beating on low speed until well blended; stir in nuts. Drop dough by rounded teaspoonfuls 2 inches apart onto prepared cookie sheets.

3. Bake 10 to 12 minutes or until edges are lightly browned. Remove to wire racks; cool completely.

4. Prepare Penuche Frosting. Frost cookies.

PENUCHE FROSTING

½ cup packed brown sugar

3 tablespoons butter

¼ cup whipping cream

1½ to 2 cups powdered sugar

1. Melt brown sugar and butter in medium saucepan over medium-high heat, stirring frequently. Bring to a boil; cook 1 minute or until slightly thickened, stirring constantly. Remove from heat; cool 10 minutes.

2. Add cream; beat until smooth. Add powdered sugar, ¼ cup at a time, beating well after each addition until frosting is desired consistency.

CHOCOLATE RASPBERRY THUMBPRINTS

Makes 4½ dozen cookies

1½ cups (3 sticks) butter, softened

1 cup granulated sugar

1 egg

1 teaspoon vanilla

3 cups all-purpose flour

¼ cup unsweetened cocoa powder

½ teaspoon salt

1 cup mini semisweet chocolate chips (optional)

Powdered sugar (optional)

⅔ cup raspberry jam

1. Preheat oven to 350°F. Line cookie sheets with parchment paper.

2. Beat butter and granulated sugar in large bowl with electric mixer at medium speed. Beat in egg and vanilla until light and fluffy. Mix in flour, cocoa and salt at low speed until well blended. Stir in mini chocolate chips, if desired.

3. Shape level tablespoonfuls of dough into balls. Place 2 inches apart on prepared cookie sheets. Make deep indentation in center of each ball with thumb.

4. Bake 12 to 15 minutes until just set. Cool on cookie sheets 2 minutes. Remove to wire racks; cool completely.

5. Sprinkle cookies with powdered sugar, if desired. Fill centers with jam. Store between layers of waxed paper in airtight containers.

TIP: If you're making these cookies as a gift, fill them with jam before baking instead of after. This will set the jam and make the cookies easier to stack and wrap.

APRICOT BISCOTTI

Makes 2½ dozen biscotti

3 cups all-purpose flour

1½ teaspoons baking soda

½ teaspoon salt

3 eggs

⅔ cup sugar

1 teaspoon vanilla

½ cup chopped dried apricots*

⅓ cup sliced almonds, chopped

1 tablespoon milk

Other chopped dried fruit such as dried cherries, cranberries or blueberries can be substituted.

1. Preheat oven to 350°F. Line cookie sheet with parchment paper. Combine flour, baking soda and salt in medium bowl.

2. Beat eggs, sugar and vanilla in large bowl with electric mixer at medium speed until blended. Add flour mixture; beat until well blended.

3. Stir in apricots and almonds. Turn out dough onto lightly floured surface. Knead four to six times. Shape dough into 20-inch log; place on prepared cookie sheet. Brush dough with milk.

4. Bake 30 minutes or until firm. Remove from oven; cool 10 minutes. Cut diagonally into 30 slices. Place slices on cookie sheet. Bake 10 minutes; turn and bake additional 10 minutes. Remove to wire rack; cool completely. Store in airtight container.

GIFT IDEAS: Make several batches of biscotti with a variety of fruit and nut combinations. Dip one end of each cookie into melted white or dark chocolate and sprinkle with toasted chopped almonds or other nuts. Let stand on parchment paper until set. Pack cookies into decorative jars or stand the cookies in an extra large mug and wrap with cellophane. Include individually wrapped tea bags, hot chocolate mix or specialty coffee.

CHOCOLATE CHERRY COOKIES

Makes 4 dozen cookies

1 package (about 16 ounces) devil's food cake mix

¾ cup (1½ sticks) butter, softened

2 eggs

1 teaspoon almond extract

24 maraschino cherries, rinsed, drained and cut into halves

¼ cup white chocolate chips

1 teaspoon canola oil

1. Preheat oven to 350°F. Line cookie sheets with parchment paper.

2. Beat cake mix, butter, eggs and almond extract in large bowl with electric mixer at low speed until crumbly. Beat at medium speed 2 minutes or until smooth dough forms. (Dough will be very sticky.)

3. Shape dough into 1-inch balls. Place 2 inches apart on prepared cookie sheets; flatten slightly. Place 1 cherry half in center of each cookie.

4. Bake 8 to 9 minutes or until cookies are no longer shiny and tops begin to crack. Cool on cookie sheets 2 minutes. Remove to wire racks; cool completely.

5. Place white chocolate chips and oil in small microwavable bowl. Microwave on HIGH 30 seconds; stir. Microwave at additional 30-second intervals, stirring after each interval, until melted and smooth. Drizzle over cookies. Let stand until set.

ELEGANT NIBBLES

TEA COOKIES

Makes 2 dozen cookies

1 cup all-purpose flour

½ cup sugar

2 tablespoons cornstarch

⅛ teaspoon salt

2 tablespoons milk

1 teaspoon vanilla

6 tablespoons butter, softened

1. Preheat oven to 350°F. Combine flour, sugar, cornstarch and salt in small bowl; mix well. Stir in milk and vanilla. Cut in butter with pastry blender or two knives until stiff dough forms.

2. Place dough between two sheets of waxed paper; roll to ⅛-inch thickness. Cut dough using 2-inch cookie cutter; place cutouts 1½ inches apart on ungreased cookie sheets. Reroll dough scraps and cut out more cookies.

3. Bake 10 to 12 minutes or until edges of cookies are lightly browned. Remove to wire racks; cool completely.

BLACK AND WHITE SANDWICH COOKIES

Makes 22 to 24 cookies

COOKIES

1¼ cups (2½ sticks) butter, softened

¾ cup superfine or granulated sugar

1 egg

1½ teaspoons vanilla

2⅓ cups all-purpose flour, divided

¼ teaspoon salt

⅓ cup unsweetened cocoa powder

FILLING

½ cup (1 stick) butter, softened

4 ounces cream cheese, softened

2 cups plus 2 tablespoons powdered sugar

2 tablespoons unsweetened cocoa powder

1. For cookies, beat 1¼ cups butter and superfine sugar in large bowl with electric mixer until creamy. Beat in egg and vanilla until well blended. Beat in 2 cups flour and salt at low speed until combined.

2. Remove half of dough to medium bowl; stir in remaining ⅓ cup flour. Add ⅓ cup cocoa to dough in mixer bowl; beat just until blended. Wrap doughs separately in plastic wrap; refrigerate 30 minutes or until firm.

3. Preheat oven to 350°F. Roll out plain dough on floured surface to ¼-inch thickness. Cut out 2-inch circles with round cookie cutters; place 2 inches apart on nonstick cookie sheet. Repeat with chocolate dough.

4. Bake 8 minutes or until firm but not browned. Remove to wire racks; cool completely.

5. For filling, beat ½ cup butter and cream cheese in medium bowl with electric mixer until well blended. Add 2 cups powdered sugar; beat until creamy. Remove half of filling to small bowl; stir in remaining 2 tablespoons powdered sugar. Add 2 tablespoons cocoa to filling in mixer bowl; beat until smooth.

6. Pipe or spread chocolate frosting on flat side of half of plain cookies; top with remaining plain cookies. Pipe or spread vanilla frosting on flat side of half of chocolate cookies; top with remaining chocolate cookies.

GIFT IDEAS: Use a 1-inch round cookie cutter to yield twice as many cookies. To make these cookies extra special, dip half of each assembled sandwich cookie into melted bittersweet or semisweet chocolate. Sprinkle with multicolored sprinkles or holiday decors. Let stand on parchment paper until set.

LEMON DROPS

Makes about 6 dozen cookies

2 cups all-purpose
   flour

⅛ teaspoon salt

1 cup (2 sticks) butter,
   softened

1 cup powdered sugar,
   divided

   Grated peel of
   1 lemon

2 teaspoons lemon
   juice

1. Preheat oven to 300°F. Combine flour and salt in medium bowl.

2. Beat butter and ¾ cup powdered sugar in large bowl with electric mixer at medium speed until fluffy. Beat in lemon peel and juice until well blended. Add flour mixture, ½ cup at a time, beating at low speed just until blended after each addition. Shape rounded teaspoonfuls of dough into balls. Place 1 inch apart on ungreased cookie sheets.

3. Bake 20 to 25 minutes or until bottoms are lightly browned. Cool on cookie sheets 5 minutes. Remove to wire racks; cool completely. Sprinkle with remaining ¼ cup powdered sugar.

PARMESAN AND PINE NUT SHORTBREAD

Makes about 2 dozen cookies

½ cup all-purpose flour

⅓ cup whole wheat flour

⅓ cup cornmeal

¼ teaspoon salt

½ cup (1 stick) butter, softened

½ cup shredded Parmesan cheese

⅓ cup sugar

¼ cup pine nuts

1. Combine all-purpose flour, whole wheat flour, cornmeal and salt in small bowl.

2. Beat butter, cheese and sugar in large bowl with electric mixer at high speed until light and fluffy. Gradually add flour mixture, beating well at low speed after each addition. Turn out dough onto lightly floured surface. Shape into 8- to 10-inch long log 2 inches in diameter. Wrap in plastic wrap; refrigerate 30 minutes.

3. Preheat oven to 375°F. Line cookie sheet with parchment paper. Cut dough into ⅓-inch slices with sharp knife. Place 1 inch apart on prepared cookie sheet. Press 3 to 5 pine nuts on each slice.

4. Bake 11 to 13 minutes or until firm and lightly browned. Cool on cookie sheet 5 minutes. Remove to wire rack; cool completely.

CHOCOLATE STRAWBERRY STACKERS

Makes about 20 cookies

1 cup (2 sticks) plus 6 tablespoons butter, softened, divided

½ cup semisweet chocolate chips, melted

2½ cups powdered sugar, divided

2 tablespoons packed brown sugar

½ teaspoon salt, divided

1 egg

2 cups all-purpose flour

⅓ cup strawberry jam

½ teaspoon vanilla

1 to 2 tablespoons milk (optional)

1. Beat 1 cup butter, melted chocolate, ½ cup powdered sugar, brown sugar and ¼ teaspoon salt in large bowl with electric mixer at medium speed 2 minutes or until light and fluffy. Add egg; beat until well blended. Add flour, ½ cup at a time, beating well at low speed after each addition.

2. Shape dough into 14-inch log. Wrap in plastic wrap; refrigerate 1 hour.

3. Preheat oven to 300°F. Cut log into ⅓-inch-thick slices; place on ungreased cookie sheets. Bake 15 to 18 minutes or until set. Cool on cookie sheets 5 minutes. Remove to wire racks; cool completely.

4. Beat remaining 6 tablespoons butter in large bowl with electric mixer at medium speed until smooth. Beat in jam, vanilla and remaining ¼ teaspoon salt until blended. Gradually add remaining 2 cups powdered sugar; beat until fluffy. If mixture is too thick, gradually beat in milk until desired spreading consistency is reached.

5. Spread frosting over flat sides of half of cookies; top with remaining cookies.

TOFFEE CREME SANDWICH COOKIES

Makes 8 cookies

1 jar (7 ounces) marshmallow creme

¾ cup toffee baking bits, divided

16 (2-inch) shortbread cookies

1. Combine marshmallow creme and ¼ cup toffee bits in medium bowl until well blended. (Mixture will be stiff.)

2. Spoon 1 teaspoon marshmallow mixture onto flat side of 1 cookie. Top with another cookie, flat side down. Roll edges in remaining ½ cup toffee bits. Repeat with remaining marshmallow creme mixture, cookies and toffee bits.

TIP: This recipe can easily be doubled or tripled. Use store-bought cookies or make your own. Try Refrigerator Cookies (page 32) or Gooey Thumbprints (page 57), minus the jam, rolled into a log, cut into ¼-inch slices and baked at 300°F 15 minutes or until set but not browned.

GINGER POLENTA COOKIES

Makes about 5 dozen cookies

2¼ cups all-purpose flour

½ cup uncooked instant polenta or yellow cornmeal

½ cup toasted pistachio nuts or pine nuts,* finely chopped

½ cup dried cranberries, finely chopped

¼ teaspoon salt

1 cup (2 sticks) butter, softened

¾ cup sugar

1 egg

1 egg yolk

½ cup finely chopped crystallized ginger

½ teaspoon ground ginger

*To toast nuts, place in single layer on ungreased baking sheet. Bake in preheated 350°F oven 8 to 10 minutes or until lightly browned, stirring occasionally.

1. Combine flour, polenta, nuts, cranberries and salt in medium bowl.

2. Beat butter and sugar in large bowl with electric mixer at medium speed until light and fluffy. Beat in egg, egg yolk, crystallized ginger and ground ginger. Add flour mixture; mix at low speed until well blended.

3. Shape dough into ball; divide in half. Roll into two 9-inch logs; wrap in plastic wrap. Roll logs to smooth surface, if necessary. Refrigerate 4 to 6 hours or until firm.

4. Preheat oven to 300°F. Line cookie sheets with parchment paper. Cut logs into ¼-inch slices; place cookies on prepared cookie sheets.

5. Bake 15 to 18 minutes or until edges are golden. Cool on cookie sheets 2 to 3 minutes. Remove to wire racks; cool completely.

CHOCOLATE HAZELNUT SANDWICH COOKIES

Makes 2½ dozen cookies

¾ cup (1½ sticks) butter, softened

¾ cup sugar

3 egg yolks

1 teaspoon vanilla

2 cups all-purpose flour

¼ teaspoon salt

⅔ cup chocolate hazelnut spread

1. Beat butter and sugar in large bowl with electric mixer at medium speed 1 minute. Beat in egg yolks and vanilla until well blended. Add flour and salt; beat at low speed just until combined. Divide dough in half. Shape each piece into 6-inch-long log 1½ inches in diameter. Wrap in plastic wrap; refrigerate at least 2 hours or until firm.

2. Preheat oven to 350°F. Line cookie sheets with parchment paper. Cut dough into ⅛-inch-thick slices; place 1 inch apart on prepared cookie sheets.

3. Bake 10 to 12 minutes or until edges are light brown. Cool on cookie sheets 5 minutes. Remove to wire racks; cool completely.

4. Spread 1 teaspoon hazelnut spread on flat side of half of cookies; top with remaining cookies. Store covered in airtight container.

ROSEMARY HONEY SHORTBREAD COOKIES

Makes 2 dozen cookies

- 2 cups all-purpose flour
- 1 tablespoon fresh rosemary leaves,* minced
- ½ teaspoon salt
- ½ teaspoon baking powder
- ¾ cup (1½ sticks) butter, softened
- ½ cup powdered sugar
- 2 tablespoons honey

For best flavor, use only fresh rosemary or substitute fresh or dried lavender buds.

1. Combine flour, rosemary, salt and baking powder in medium bowl.

2. Beat butter, powdered sugar and honey in large bowl with electric mixer at medium speed until creamy. Beat in flour mixture at low speed just until blended. (Mixture will be crumbly.) Shape dough into log. Wrap in plastic wrap; refrigerate 1 hour or until firm. (Dough can be refrigerated several days before baking.)

3. Preheat oven to 350°F. Line cookie sheets with parchment paper. Cut log into ½-inch slices. Place 2 inches apart on prepared cookie sheets.

4. Bake 13 minutes or until set. Cool on cookie sheets 1 minute. Remove to wire racks; cool completely.

CHOCOLATE ALMOND MERINGUE SANDWICH COOKIES

Makes 16 cookies

½ cup sugar, divided

¼ cup ground almonds

1 tablespoon unsweetened cocoa powder

1 teaspoon cornstarch

2 egg whites

⅛ teaspoon cream of tartar

¼ teaspoon almond extract

⅓ cup chocolate fudge topping

1. Preheat oven to 250°F. Line cookie sheets with foil; spray foil with nonstick cooking spray. Combine 3 tablespoons sugar, almonds, cocoa and cornstarch in small bowl.

2. Beat egg whites in medium bowl with electric mixer at medium speed until foamy. Add cream of tartar; beat at high speed until soft peaks form. Gradually add almond extract and remaining sugar; beat at high speed until stiff peaks form. Gently fold cocoa mixture into egg whites.

3. Drop rounded teaspoonfuls of meringue mixture about 2 inches apart onto prepared cookie sheets. (Or mixture may be piped using piping bag fitted with large tip.)

4. Bake 40 minutes. Cool cookies on cookie sheets 2 minutes; use thin spatula to loosen cookies from foil. Remove to wire racks; cool completely.

5. Spread 1 teaspoon fudge topping on flat side of half of cookies; top with remaining cookies. Store cookies in airtight container up to 2 days.

BUTTERY LEMONGRASS WEDGES

Makes 2 dozen cookies

1 cup sliced almonds with skins, toasted and cooled

¾ cup superfine or granulated sugar

¼ cup lemongrass purée*

Grated peel of 2 large lemons

½ teaspoon salt

1¼ cups all-purpose flour

¾ cup (1½ sticks) cold butter, cut into small pieces

2 teaspoons vanilla

Powdered sugar (optional)

Lemongrass purée can be found in the refrigerated produce section of well-stocked supermarkets or at Asian specialty markets.

1. Pulse almonds in food processor. Add sugar, lemongrass, lemon peel and salt; pulse until finely ground. Add flour; pulse until combined. Add butter and vanilla. Pulse just until large clumps form. *Do not overprocess.*

2. Spray two 9-inch springform pans with nonstick cooking spray. Divide dough in half and pat evenly into pans. Cover with plastic wrap; refrigerate 3 to 4 hours or overnight.

3. Preheat oven to 325°F. Bake 20 to 23 minutes or until golden brown. Cool 10 minutes. Remove sides of springform pans and cut each circle into 12 wedges. Cool completely. Sprinkle with powdered sugar, if desired.

MINI LEMON SANDWICH COOKIES

Makes 4½ dozen cookies

2 cups all-purpose flour

1¼ cups (2½ sticks) butter, softened, divided

½ cup granulated sugar, divided

⅓ cup whipping cream

1 teaspoon grated lemon peel

⅛ teaspoon lemon extract

¾ cup powdered sugar

2 to 3 teaspoons lemon juice

1 teaspoon vanilla

Yellow food coloring (optional)

1. For cookies, combine flour, 1 cup butter, ¼ cup granulated sugar, cream, lemon peel and lemon extract in large bowl. Beat with electric mixer at medium speed 2 to 3 minutes or until well blended. Divide dough into thirds. Wrap each piece in waxed paper; refrigerate until firm.

2. Preheat oven to 375°F. Place remaining ¼ cup granulated sugar in shallow bowl. Roll out each piece of dough to ⅛-inch thickness on floured surface. Cut out dough with 1½-inch round cookie cutter. Dip both sides of each cookie in sugar. Place 1 inch apart on ungreased cookie sheets; pierce several times with fork.

3. Bake 6 to 9 minutes or until cookies are slightly puffed but not brown. Cool on cookie sheets 1 minute. Remove to wire racks; cool completely.

4. For filling, beat powdered sugar, remaining ¼ cup butter, lemon juice and vanilla in large bowl with electric mixer at medium speed 1 to 2 minutes or until smooth. Tint with food coloring, if desired. Spread ½ teaspoon filling each on flat side of half of cookies; top with remaining cookies.

YULETIDE BARS AND BROWNIES

TOFFEE BARS

Makes 2 to 3 dozen bars

½ cup (1 stick) butter, softened

½ cup packed brown sugar

1 egg yolk

1 teaspoon vanilla

1 cup all-purpose flour

1 cup milk chocolate chips

½ cup chopped walnuts or pecans

1. Preheat oven to 350°F. Spray 13×9-inch baking pan with nonstick cooking spray.

2. Beat butter and brown sugar in large bowl with electric mixer at medium speed until creamy. Blend in egg yolk and vanilla. Stir in flour until well blended. Press dough into prepared pan.

3. Bake 15 minutes or until golden. Sprinkle evenly with chocolate chips. Let stand several minutes until chips melt; spread chocolate evenly over bars. Sprinkle with walnuts. Score into bars while still warm. Cool completely in pan on wire rack; cut into bars along score lines.

CHOCOLATE CHIP SOUR CREAM BROWNIES

Makes 2 to 3 dozen brownies

½ cup (1 stick) butter, softened

1 cup packed brown sugar

1 cup sour cream

1 egg

1 teaspoon vanilla

½ cup unsweetened cocoa powder

½ teaspoon baking soda

¼ teaspoon salt

2 cups all-purpose flour

1 cup semisweet chocolate chips

Powdered sugar (optional)

1. Preheat oven to 350°F. Spray 13×9-inch baking pan with nonstick cooking spray.

2. Beat butter and brown sugar in large bowl with electric mixer until creamy. Add sour cream, egg and vanilla; beat until light and fluffy. Add cocoa, baking soda and salt; beat until smooth. Gradually beat in flour at low speed until well blended. Stir in chocolate chips. Spread batter evenly in prepared pan.

3. Bake 25 to 30 minutes or until toothpick inserted into center comes out clean and center springs back when touched. Cool completely in pan on wire rack. Sprinkle with powdered sugar, if desired. Cut into bars.

CHOCOLATE CARAMEL BARS

Makes 2 to 3 dozen bars

2 cups all-purpose flour

1½ cups packed brown sugar, divided

1¼ cups (2½ sticks) butter, softened, divided

1 cup chopped pecans

1 cup semisweet chocolate chips

1. Preheat oven to 350°F.

2. Combine flour, 1 cup brown sugar and ½ cup butter in large bowl until crumbly. Press firmly into 13×9-inch baking pan; sprinkle pecans evenly over top.

3. Combine remaining ½ cup brown sugar and ¾ cup butter in medium heavy saucepan. Cook over medium heat until mixture comes to a boil, stirring constantly. Boil 1 minute, stirring constantly. Pour caramel evenly over pecans and crust.

4. Bake 18 to 20 minutes or until caramel layer bubbles evenly all over. Immediately sprinkle with chocolate chips. Let stand 2 minutes or until chips melt; spread chocolate evenly over bars. Let stand until chocolate is set; cut into bars.

CARAMEL BACON NUT BROWNIES

Makes 2 to 3 dozen brownies

¾ cup (1½ sticks) butter

4 ounces unsweetened chocolate, chopped

2 cups sugar

4 eggs

1 cup all-purpose flour

1 package (14 ounces) caramels

¼ cup whipping cream

2 cups pecan halves or coarsely chopped pecans, divided

4 slices bacon, crisp-cooked and crumbled

1 package (12 ounces) chocolate chunks or chips, divided

1. Preheat oven to 350°F. Spray 13×9-inch baking pan with nonstick cooking spray.

2. Place butter and chocolate in large microwavable bowl. Microwave on HIGH 1½ to 2 minutes or until melted and smooth, stirring at 30-second intervals. Stir in sugar. Add eggs, one at a time, beating until blended after each addition. Stir in flour. Spread half of batter in prepared pan. Bake 20 minutes.

3. Meanwhile, combine caramels and cream in medium microwavable bowl. Microwave on HIGH 1½ to 2 minutes or until caramels begin to melt; stir until smooth. Stir in 1 cup pecan halves and bacon.

4. Spread caramel mixture over partially baked brownie layer. Sprinkle with half of chocolate chunks. Pour remaining brownie batter over top; sprinkle with remaining 1 cup pecan halves and chocolate chunks.

5. Bake 25 minutes or until set. Cool completely in pan on wire rack. Cut into squares.

WHITE CHOCOLATE PEPPERMINT BROWNIES

Makes 12 to 16 brownies

BROWNIES

1 package (12 ounces) white chocolate chips, divided

¼ cup granulated sugar

3 eggs

1 cup all-purpose flour

½ cup (1 stick) butter, softened

½ teaspoon salt

½ cup chopped peppermint candies

FROSTING

1¼ cups powdered sugar

6 tablespoons butter, softened

3 tablespoons cream cheese

Crushed peppermint candies

1. Preheat oven to 350°F. Spray 9-inch square baking pan with nonstick cooking spray.

2. Melt half of white chocolate chips in small saucepan over very low heat, stirring constantly until smooth. Cool slightly.

3. Beat granulated sugar and eggs in large bowl with electric mixer at medium-high speed 5 minutes. Add melted chocolate, flour, ½ cup butter and salt; beat on low speed until blended. Stir in chopped peppermints. Spread batter in prepared pan.

4. Bake 20 to 25 minutes or until toothpick inserted into center comes out clean. Cool completely in pan on wire rack.

5. Meanwhile for frosting, melt remaining half of white chocolate chips in small saucepan over very low heat, stirring constantly until smooth. Cool slightly. Beat powdered sugar, 6 tablespoons butter and cream cheese and in large bowl with electric mixer until smooth. Beat in melted chocolate. Spread over brownies; sprinkle with crushed peppermint candies.

TANGY LEMON RASPBERRY BARS

Makes 12 to 16 bars

¾ cup packed brown sugar

½ cup (1 stick) butter, softened

Grated peel of 1 lemon

1 cup all-purpose flour

1 cup old-fashioned oats

1 teaspoon baking powder

½ teaspoon salt

½ cup raspberry jam

1. Preheat oven to 350°F. Spray 8-inch square baking pan with nonstick cooking spray.

2. Beat brown sugar, butter and lemon peel in large bowl with electric mixer at medium speed until combined. Add flour, oats, baking powder and salt; beat at low speed until combined. Reserve ¼ cup mixture. Press remaining mixture into prepared pan. Spread jam over top; sprinkle with reserved mixture.

3. Bake 25 minutes or until edges are lightly browned. Cool completely in pan on wire rack. Cut into bars.

HAWAIIAN BARS

Makes 12 to 16 bars

1⅓ cups all-purpose flour

1 teaspoon baking powder

¼ teaspoon baking soda

¼ teaspoon salt

10 tablespoons (1¼ sticks) butter

1 teaspoon vanilla

2 eggs

1 cup packed dark brown sugar

¾ cup coarsely chopped salted macadamia nuts

¾ cup flaked coconut

⅓ cup granulated sugar

1. Preheat oven to 350°F. Spray 9-inch square baking pan with nonstick cooking spray. Whisk flour, baking powder, baking soda and salt in medium bowl.

2. Melt butter in large heavy saucepan over low heat. Remove from heat; stir in vanilla. Beat in eggs, one at a time. Add flour mixture, brown sugar, nuts, coconut and granulated sugar; mix well. Spread batter in prepared pan.

3. Bake 30 minutes or until edges begin to pull away from sides of pan. Cool completely in pan on wire rack. Cut into bars. Store in airtight container.

NOTE: Bars firm up and taste even better the day after they're made.

FRUIT AND PECAN BROWNIES

Makes 12 to 16 brownies

2 ounces unsweetened chocolate, chopped

1 cup sugar

½ cup (1 stick) butter, softened

2 eggs

1 teaspoon vanilla

1 cup chopped dried mixed fruit

½ cup all-purpose flour

1 cup coarsely chopped pecans, divided

1 cup semisweet chocolate chips, divided

1. Preheat oven to 350°F. Spray 8-inch square baking pan with nonstick cooking spray. Melt unsweetened chocolate in top of double boiler over simmering water. Remove from heat; cool slightly.

2. Beat sugar and butter in large bowl with electric mixer at medium speed until light and fluffy. Add eggs, one at a time, beating until blended after each addition. Beat in chocolate and vanilla. Stir in fruit, flour, ½ cup pecans and ½ cup chocolate chips. Spread batter in prepared pan. Sprinkle with remaining ½ cup pecans and ½ cup chocolate chips.

3. Bake 25 to 30 minutes or just until center feels firm. *Do not overbake*. Remove from oven; cover warm bars with waxed paper or foil. Cool completely in pan on wire rack. Cut into squares.

CHERRY CHEESECAKE SWIRL BARS

Makes 12 to 16 bars

1⅔ cups shortbread cookie crumbs

½ cup (1 stick) butter, melted

¾ cup sugar, divided

2 packages (8 ounces each) cream cheese, softened

3 eggs

½ cup sour cream

½ teaspoon almond extract

3 tablespoons strained cherry preserves, melted

1. Preheat oven to 325°F.

2. Combine cookie crumbs, butter and ¼ cup sugar in medium bowl; mix well. Press mixture into 9-inch square baking pan. Bake 10 minutes or until set but not browned. Cool completely.

3. Beat cream cheese in large bowl with electric mixer at medium speed until fluffy. Add remaining ½ cup sugar; beat until smooth. Add eggs, one at a time, beating well after each addition. Add sour cream and almond extract; beat until well blended. Spread evenly in prepared crust.

4. Drizzle melted preserves over cheesecake batter. Drag tip of knife through jam and batter to swirl.

5. Place pan in 13×9-inch baking dish; add water to come halfway up sides of cheesecake.

6. Bake 45 to 50 minutes or until knife inserted 1 inch from edge comes out clean. Cool completely in pan on wire rack. Cover and refrigerate 2 hours or until ready to serve.

DULCE DE LECHE BLONDIES

Makes 2 to 3 dozen bars

2 cups all-purpose flour

1 teaspoon baking soda

1 teaspoon salt

1 cup (2 sticks) butter, softened

1 cup packed brown sugar

2 eggs

1½ teaspoons vanilla

1 package (14 ounces) caramels

½ cup evaporated milk

1. Preheat oven to 350°F. Spray 13×9-inch baking pan with nonstick cooking spray. Whisk flour, baking soda and salt in medium bowl.

2. Beat butter and brown sugar in large bowl with electric mixer at medium speed until creamy. Add eggs, one at a time, beating well after each addition. Beat in vanilla. Gradually add flour mixture; beat just until blended. Spread half of batter in prepared pan. Bake 8 minutes. Cool in pan on wire rack 5 minutes.

3. Meanwhile, melt caramels with evaporated milk in small saucepan over low heat; reserve 2 tablespoons. Pour remaining caramel mixture over baked bottom layer. Drop tablespoonfuls of remaining batter over caramel layer; swirl slightly with knife.

4. Bake 25 minutes or until golden brown. Cool completely in pan on wire rack. Cut into squares. Reheat reserved caramel, if necessary; drizzle over bars.

SHORTBREAD TURTLE COOKIE BARS

Makes 2 to 3 dozen bars

1¼ cups (2½ sticks) butter, softened, divided

1 cup all-purpose flour

1 cup old-fashioned oats

1½ cups packed brown sugar, divided

1 teaspoon ground cinnamon

¼ teaspoon salt

1½ cups chopped pecans

6 ounces bittersweet or semisweet chocolate, finely chopped

4 ounces white chocolate, finely chopped

1. Preheat oven to 350°F.

2. Beat ½ cup butter with electric mixer at medium speed 2 minutes or until light and fluffy. Add flour, oats, ¾ cup brown sugar, cinnamon and salt; beat at low speed until coarse crumbs form. Press firmly into ungreased 13×9-inch baking pan.

3. Combine remaining ¾ cup butter and ¾ cup brown sugar in heavy medium saucepan. Cook over medium heat, stirring constantly until mixture comes to a boil. Boil 1 minute without stirring. Remove from heat; stir in pecans. Pour evenly over crust.

4. Bake 18 to 22 minutes or until caramel begins to bubble. Immediately sprinkle with bittersweet and white chocolates; let stand 1 minute or until softened. Swirl with knife. Cool completely in pan on wire rack; cut into bars.

CHEWY PEANUT BUTTER BROWNIES

Makes 2 to 3 dozen brownies

¾ cup (1½ sticks) butter, melted

¾ cup creamy peanut butter

1¾ cups sugar

2 teaspoons vanilla

4 eggs, lightly beaten

1¼ cups all-purpose flour

½ teaspoon baking powder

¼ teaspoon salt

¼ cup unsweetened cocoa powder

1. Preheat oven to 350°F. Spray 13×9-inch baking pan with nonstick cooking spray.

2. Beat butter and peanut butter in large bowl with electric mixer at low speed 3 minutes or until well blended. Beat in sugar and vanilla until blended. Add eggs, one at a time, beating until well blended after each addition. Stir in flour, baking powder and salt just until blended. Reserve 1¾ cups batter. Stir cocoa into remaining batter.

3. Spread chocolate batter in prepared pan. Top with reserved batter. Bake 30 minutes or until edges begin to pull away from sides of pan. Cool completely in pan on wire rack. Cut into bars.

INTERNATIONAL CHEER

CHINESE ALMOND COOKIES

Makes about 2½ dozen cookies

1 package (about 16 ounces) yellow cake mix

5 tablespoons butter, melted

1 egg

1½ teaspoons almond extract

30 whole almonds

1 egg yolk

1 teaspoon water

1. Beat cake mix, butter, egg and almond extract in large bowl with electric mixer at medium speed until well blended. Shape dough into disc. Wrap in plastic wrap; refrigerate 4 hours or overnight.

2. Preheat oven to 350°F. Line cookie sheets with parchment paper.

3. Shape dough into 1-inch balls; place 2 inches apart on prepared cookie sheets. Press 1 almond into center of each ball, flattening slightly. Whisk egg yolk and water in small bowl. Brush tops of cookies with egg yolk mixture.

4. Bake 10 to 12 minutes or until lightly browned. Cool on cookie sheets 5 minutes. Remove to wire racks; cool completely.

CHOCOLATE-FROSTED LEBKUCHEN

Makes about 6 dozen cookies

1 cup sugar

4 eggs

1½ cups all-purpose flour

1 cup (6 ounces) ground almonds*

⅓ cup candied lemon peel, finely chopped

⅓ cup candied orange peel, finely chopped

1½ teaspoons ground cinnamon

1 teaspoon grated lemon peel

½ teaspoon ground cardamom

½ teaspoon ground nutmeg

¼ teaspoon ground cloves

3 ounces bittersweet or semisweet chocolate, coarsely chopped

1 tablespoon butter

To grind almonds, place in food processor or blender. Pulse until finely ground but not pasty.

1. Beat sugar and eggs in large bowl with electric mixer at high speed 10 minutes.

2. Meanwhile, combine flour, almonds, candied lemon and orange peels, cinnamon, grated lemon peel, cardamom, nutmeg and cloves in another large bowl. Add egg mixture; stir until well blended. Cover; refrigerate 12 hours or overnight.

3. Preheat oven to 350°F. Line cookie sheets with parchment paper. Drop dough by rounded teaspoonfuls 2 inches apart onto prepared cookie sheets. Bake 8 to 10 minutes or just until browned. *Do not overbake.* Remove to wire racks; cool slightly.

4. Meanwhile, combine chocolate and butter in small microwavable bowl. Microwave on HIGH 30 seconds; stir. Repeat until chocolate is melted and mixture is smooth. Spread over tops of warm cookies. Let stand until glaze is set. Store in airtight container.

ARGENTINEAN CARAMEL–FILLED CRESCENTS (PASTELES)

Makes about 4 dozen cookies

3 cups all-purpose flour

½ cup powdered sugar

1 teaspoon baking powder

¼ teaspoon salt

1 cup (2 sticks) butter, cut into small pieces

6 to 7 tablespoons ice water

½ package (14 ounces) caramels

2 tablespoons milk

½ cup flaked coconut

1 egg

1 tablespoon water

1. Combine flour, powdered sugar, baking powder and salt in large bowl. Cut in butter with pastry blender or two knives until mixture forms pea-sized pieces. Add water, 1 tablespoon at a time; toss with fork until mixture holds together. Divide dough in half. Wrap separately in plastic wrap; refrigerate 30 minutes or until firm.

2. Meanwhile, melt caramels and milk in medium saucepan over low heat, stirring constantly; stir in coconut. Remove from heat; cool.

3. Roll out dough on lightly floured surface to ¼-inch thickness. Cut dough with 3-inch round cookie cutter. Gather and reroll scraps; cut additional circles.

4. Preheat oven to 400°F. Line cookie sheets with parchment paper. Beat egg and water in cup. Place ½ teaspoon caramel mixture in center of each dough round. Moisten edge of dough round with egg mixture. Fold dough in half; press edges firmly to seal in filling. Press edges with fork. Place crescents on prepared cookie sheets; brush with egg mixture. Cut 3 slashes across top of each cookie with tip of knife.

5. Bake 15 to 20 minutes or until golden brown. Remove cookies to wire racks; cool completely. Store tightly covered at room temperature.

QUEBEC MAPLE–PECAN DROPS

Makes about 2 dozen cookies

COOKIES

- 1 cup all-purpose flour
- ½ teaspoon baking soda
- ¼ teaspoon salt
- ½ cup (1 stick) butter, softened
- ½ cup granulated sugar
- 3 tablespoons maple syrup
- 1 cup quick oats*
- ½ cup coarsely chopped pecans, toasted**
- ¼ cup chopped pitted dates

FROSTING

- 2 ounces cream cheese, softened
- 2 tablespoons butter, softened
- 2 tablespoons maple syrup
- 1½ cups powdered sugar
- ⅓ cup finely chopped pecans, toasted

*Do not use old-fashioned oats.
**To toast pecans, spread in single layer on baking sheet. Bake in preheated 350°F oven 5 to 7 minutes or until lightly toasted, stirring frequently.*

1. Preheat oven to 350°F. Combine flour, baking soda and salt in medium bowl.

2. Beat ½ cup butter and granulated sugar in large bowl with electric mixer at medium speed until creamy. Beat in 3 tablespoons syrup. Gradually beat in flour mixture, oats, coarsely chopped pecans and dates at low speed. Drop dough by rounded tablespoonfuls 2 inches apart onto ungreased cookie sheets.

3. Bake 12 minutes or until cookies are golden brown. Cool on cookie sheets 2 minutes. Remove to wire racks; cool completely.

4. For frosting, beat cream cheese and 2 tablespoons butter in large bowl with electric mixer at medium speed until smooth. Beat in 2 tablespoons syrup. Gradually beat in powdered sugar until smooth. Spread frosting over cooled cookies; top with finely chopped pecans.

BOLIVIAN ALMOND COOKIES (ALFAJORES DE ALMENDRAS)

Makes about 3 dozen cookies

4 cups whole almonds

1 cup all-purpose flour

¼ teaspoon salt

1 cup sugar

¾ cup (1½ sticks) butter, softened

1 teaspoon vanilla

½ teaspoon almond extract

2 eggs

2 tablespoons milk

1 tablespoon grated lemon peel

1 cup sliced almonds

1. Preheat oven to 350°F. Line cookie sheets with parchment paper.

2. Place whole almonds in food processor. Pulse until almonds are ground but not pasty.

3. Combine ground almonds, flour and salt in medium bowl.

4. Beat sugar, butter, vanilla and almond extract in large bowl with electric mixer at medium speed until light and fluffy. Beat in eggs and milk. Gradually add half of flour mixture at low speed until well blended. Stir in lemon peel and remaining flour mixture.

5. Drop rounded teaspoonfuls of dough 2 inches apart onto prepared cookie sheets. Flatten slightly with spoon; top with sliced almonds.

6. Bake 10 to 12 minutes or until edges are lightly browned. Remove to wire racks; cool completely.

BELGIAN TUILE COOKIES

Makes about 2½ dozen cookies

½ cup (1 stick) butter, softened

½ cup sugar

1 egg white

1 teaspoon vanilla

¼ teaspoon salt

½ cup all-purpose flour

4 ounces bittersweet chocolate, chopped or semisweet chocolate chips

1. Preheat oven to 375°F. Line cookie sheets with parchment paper.

2. Beat butter and sugar in large bowl with electric mixer at medium speed until light and fluffy. Beat in egg white, vanilla and salt. Gradually add flour at low speed until well blended. Drop rounded teaspoonfuls of batter 4 inches apart onto prepared cookie sheets. (Bake only 4 cookies per sheet.) Flatten slightly with spatula.

3. Bake 6 to 8 minutes or until cookies are deep golden brown. Let cookies stand on cookie sheet 1 minute. Working quickly while cookies are still hot, drape cookies over rolling pin or bottle to form saddle shape; cool completely.

4. Melt chocolate in small heavy saucepan over low heat, stirring constantly.

5. Tilt saucepan to pool chocolate at one end; dip edge of each cookie, turning slowly so entire edge is tinged with chocolate.

6. Transfer cookies to waxed paper; let stand at room temperature 1 hour or until set. Store tightly covered at room temperature. Do not freeze.

FESTIVE LEBKUCHEN

Makes 2 dozen cookies

3 tablespoons butter

1 cup packed brown sugar

¼ cup honey

1 egg
Grated peel and juice of 1 lemon

3 cups all-purpose flour

2 teaspoons ground allspice

½ teaspoon baking soda

½ teaspoon salt

Royal Icing (recipe follows, or page 141)

1. Combine butter, brown sugar and honey in medium saucepan; cook over low heat until butter is melted, stirring constantly. Pour into large bowl; cool 30 minutes.

2. Add egg, lemon peel and lemon juice; beat with electric mixer at high speed 2 minutes. Stir in flour, allspice, baking soda and salt until well blended. Cover; refrigerate overnight or up to 3 days.

3. Preheat oven to 350°F. Line cookie sheets with parchment paper. Roll out dough to ½-inch thickness on lightly floured surface with lightly floured rolling pin. Cut dough with desired cookie cutters; place on prepared cookie sheets.

4. Bake 15 to 18 minutes until edges are lightly browned. Cool on cookie sheets 1 minute. Remove to wire racks; cool completely. Decorate with white frosting. Store in airtight container.

ROYAL ICING: Combine 4 cups powdered sugar, 6 tablespoons water and 3 tablespoons meringue powder in medium bowl. Beat with electric mixer at high speed 7 to 10 minutes or until soft peaks form. Cover surface with plastic wrap until needed. Makes about 2 cups.

OLD WORLD PFEFFERNÜSSE COOKIES

Makes about 4 dozen cookies

¾ cup packed brown sugar

½ cup (1 stick) butter, softened

½ cup molasses

1 egg

1 tablespoon licorice-flavored liqueur (optional)

3¼ cups all-purpose flour

1 teaspoon baking soda

1 teaspoon ground cinnamon

½ teaspoon ground cloves

¼ teaspoon ground nutmeg

Dash black pepper

Powdered sugar (optional)

1. Preheat oven to 350°F. Line cookie sheets with parchment paper.

2. Beat brown sugar and butter in large bowl with electric mixer at medium speed until creamy. Beat in molasses, egg and liqueur, if desired, until light and fluffy. Mix in flour, baking soda, cinnamon, cloves, nutmeg and pepper at low speed until well blended. Shape level tablespoonfuls of dough into balls. Place 2 inches apart on prepared cookie sheets.

3. Bake 12 to 14 minutes or until set. Cool on cookie sheets 2 minutes. Remove to wire racks; cool completely. Sprinkle with powdered sugar, if desired. Store in airtight containers.

HUNGARIAN LEMON POPPY SEED COOKIES

Makes about 2 dozen cookies

1¼ cups all-purpose flour

½ teaspoon baking soda

¼ teaspoon salt

⅔ cup granulated sugar

½ cup (1 stick) butter, softened

1 egg

2 teaspoons grated lemon peel

1 tablespoon poppy seeds

1 cup powdered sugar

2 tablespoons lemon juice

1. Preheat oven to 350°F. Combine flour, baking soda and salt in medium bowl.

2. For cookies, beat granulated sugar and butter in large bowl of electric mixer at medium speed until creamy. Beat in egg and lemon peel. Gradually add flour mixture and poppy seeds at low speed. Drop dough by heaping teaspoonfuls 2 inches apart onto ungreased cookie sheets.

3. Bake 11 to 12 minutes or until edges are lightly browned. Cool on cookie sheets 1 minute. Remove to wire racks; cool completely.

4. For glaze, combine powdered sugar and lemon juice in small bowl; mix well. Drizzle glaze over cookies; let stand about 20 minutes or until glaze is set.

PEBBERNODDERS

Makes about 16 dozen small cookies

3 cups all-purpose flour

1 teaspoon baking powder

1 teaspoon ground cinnamon

½ teaspoon ground ginger

½ teaspoon ground cloves

1½ cups sugar

1½ cups (3 sticks) butter, softened

3 eggs

2 teaspoons freshly grated lemon peel

1. Combine flour, baking powder, cinnamon, ginger and cloves in medium bowl.

2. Beat sugar and butter in large bowl with electric mixer at medium speed until creamy. Add eggs and lemon peel; beat until well blended. Gradually add flour mixture at low speed just until blended.

3. Line cookie sheets with parchment paper. Divide dough into four equal pieces; shape each piece into ¾-inch-thick rope about 12 inches long. Place ropes on prepared cookie sheets. Freeze about 30 minutes or until firm.

4. Preheat oven to 375°F. Cut frozen ropes into ¼-inch-thick slices; place 1 inch apart on prepared cookie sheets. Bake 10 to 12 minutes or until lightly browned. Remove to wire racks; cool completely.

HAZELNUT BISCOTTI

Makes about 2 dozen biscotti

4 cups all-purpose flour

2 cups sugar

4 teaspoons baking powder

6 eggs

¼ cup hazelnut liqueur

2 teaspoons almond extract

2 teaspoons vanilla

2 cups toasted hazelnuts, chopped*

1 cup white chocolate chips, melted (optional)

2 tablespoons very finely chopped hazelnuts (optional)

*To toast nuts, spread in single layer on baking sheet. Bake in preheated 350°F oven 8 to 10 minutes or until golden brown, stirring frequently.

1. Preheat oven to 350°F. Line cookie sheets with parchment paper.

2. Combine flour, sugar and baking powder in medium bowl.

3. Beat eggs, liqueur, almond extract and vanilla in large bowl with electric mixer on high speed until frothy. Stir into flour mixture until well blended. Add nuts; knead gently four to five times until nuts are evenly distributed. Divide dough in half. Shape each half into 3-inch-wide flat loaves on prepared cookie sheets.

4. Bake 20 minutes until loaves are solid and sound hollow when tapped. Remove to wire racks; cool completely.

5. Cut in ¾-inch-thick slices. Place slices, cut side up, on prepared cookie sheets. Bake 15 minutes or until golden brown. Remove to wire racks; cool completely.

6. Dip one end of each cookie in melted white chocolate and sprinkle with finely chopped hazelnuts, if desired. Let stand on parchment paper until set.

FINNISH SPICE COOKIES (NISSU NASSU)

Makes about 5 dozen cookies

2 cups all-purpose flour

1½ teaspoons ground ginger

1½ teaspoons ground cinnamon

½ teaspoon ground cardamom

½ teaspoon ground cloves

⅔ cup packed brown sugar

½ cup (1 stick) butter, softened

½ teaspoon baking soda

3 to 5 tablespoons hot water

Royal Icing (recipe follows, or page 130)

1. Combine flour, ginger, cinnamon, cardamom and cloves in medium bowl.

2. Beat brown sugar and butter in large bowl with electric mixer at medium-high speed until light and fluffy. Stir baking soda into 3 tablespoons hot water in small bowl until dissolved. Beat into butter mixture. Gradually add flour mixture at low speed until dough forms. (If dough is too crumbly, add additional hot water, 1 tablespoon at a time, until dough holds together.) Shape dough into two discs. Wrap separately in plastic wrap; refrigerate 30 minutes or until firm.

3. Preheat oven to 375°F. Line cookie sheets with parchment paper.

4. Working with one disc at a time, roll out dough on lightly floured surface to ⅛-inch thickness. Cut dough with floured 3-inch pig-shaped cookie cutter or desired cookie cutter. Place cutouts 1 inch apart on prepared cookie sheets. Gather scraps and reroll; cut additional cookies.

5. Bake 8 to 10 minutes or until firm and edges are lightly browned. Remove to wire racks; cool completely.

6. Prepare Royal Icing. Spoon icing into pastry bag fitted with writing tip. Decorate cooled cookies with icing. Let stand 1 hour or until set. Store tightly covered at room temperature or freeze up to 3 months.

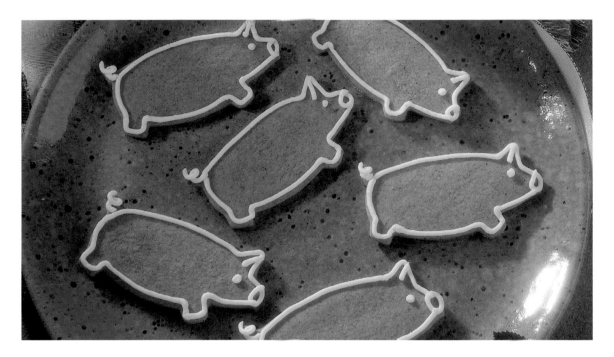

ROYAL ICING

1 **egg white,* at room temperature**

2 **to 2½ cups sifted powdered sugar**

½ **teaspoon almond extract**

*Use only grade A clean, uncracked egg.

1. Beat egg white in small bowl at high speed of electric mixture until foamy.

2. Gradually add 2 cups powdered sugar and almond extract at low speed until moistened. Increase speed to high; beat until icing is stiff.

SPUMONE BARS

Makes 4 dozen cookies

¾ cup (1½ sticks) butter, softened

⅔ cup sugar

3 egg yolks

1 teaspoon vanilla

¼ teaspoon baking powder

⅛ teaspoon salt

2 cups all-purpose flour

12 maraschino cherries, well drained and chopped

¼ cup chopped walnuts

¼ cup mint-flavored or plain semisweet chocolate chips

2 teaspoons water, divided

1. Preheat oven to 350°F. Beat butter and sugar in large bowl with electric mixer at medium-high speed until blended. Beat in egg yolks, vanilla, baking powder and salt until light and fluffy. Add flour at low speed until stiff dough forms.

2. Divide dough into three equal parts; place each part in separate small bowl. Add cherries and walnuts to one part; mix well. Melt chocolate chips in small saucepan over low heat, stirring constantly. Add melted chocolate and 1 teaspoon water to second part, mix well. Stir remaining 1 teaspoon water into third part. (If doughs are soft, refrigerate 10 minutes.)

3. Divide each color of dough into four equal pieces; roll each piece into 6-inch rope on lightly floured surface. Place one rope of each color side by side on ungreased cookie sheet. Flatten ropes so they attach together making one strip of three colors. With rolling pin, roll strip directly on cookie sheet until it measures 12×3 inches. With straight edge of knife, score strip crosswise at 1-inch intervals. Repeat with remaining ropes.

4. Bake 12 to 13 minutes or until set but not browned. While cookies are still warm, trim lengthwise edges to make them even and cut into individual cookies along score marks. Cool completely on cookie sheets.

DANISH COOKIE RINGS (VANILLEKRANSER)

Makes about 5 dozen cookies

½ cup blanched almonds

2 cups all-purpose flour

¾ cup sugar

¼ teaspoon baking powder

1 cup (2 sticks) butter, cut into small pieces

1 egg

1 tablespoon milk

1 tablespoon vanilla

15 candied red cherries

15 candied green cherries

1. Pulse almonds in food processor until finely ground, but not pasty. Place almonds, flour, sugar and baking powder in large bowl. Cut in butter with pastry blender or two knives until mixture is crumbly.

2. Beat egg, milk and vanilla in small bowl until well blended. Add egg mixture to flour mixture; stir until soft dough forms.

3. Line cookie sheets with parchment paper. Spoon dough into pastry bag fitted with medium star tip. Pipe 3-inch rings 2 inches apart on prepared cookie sheets. Refrigerate 15 minutes or until firm.

4. Preheat oven to 375°F. Cut red cherries into quarters. Cut green cherries into halves; cut each half into four slivers. Press red cherry quarter onto each ring where ends meet. Place green cherry sliver on either side of red cherry to form leaves.

5. Bake 8 to 10 minutes or until golden. Remove to wire racks; cool completely. Store tightly covered at room temperature or freeze up to 3 months.

SANTA'S FAVORITE COOKIES

FESTIVE CANDY CANES

Makes about 2 dozen cookies

1 cup powdered sugar

¾ cup (1½ sticks) butter, softened

1 egg

1 teaspoon peppermint extract

½ teaspoon vanilla

1⅔ to 1¾ cups all-purpose flour

⅛ teaspoon salt

Red food coloring

1. Preheat oven to 350°F. Beat powdered sugar and butter in large bowl with electric mixer at medium speed until light and fluffy. Add egg, peppermint extract and vanilla; beat until well blended. Add flour and salt; beat until well blended. (Dough will be sticky.)

2. Divide dough in half. Tint half of dough with food coloring to desired shade of red. Leave remaining dough plain. For each candy cane, roll heaping teaspoonful red and plain dough into separate 5-inch ropes with floured hands. Twist ropes together; bend into candy cane shape. Place 2 inches apart on ungreased cookie sheets.

3. Bake 7 to 8 minutes or until set and edges are lightly browned. Cool on cookie sheets 2 minutes. Remove to wire racks; cool completely.

EGGNOG SANDWICH COOKIES

Makes about 6 dozen cookies

COOKIES

2½ cups all-purpose flour

¼ teaspoon salt

1 cup (2 sticks) butter, softened

1¼ cups plus 1 tablespoon granulated sugar, divided

1 egg yolk

½ cup sour cream

½ teaspoon ground nutmeg

¼ teaspoon ground ginger

FILLING

½ cup (1 stick) butter, softened

¼ cup shortening

2½ cups powdered sugar

2 tablespoons brandy or milk

1. Preheat oven to 350°F. Line cookie sheets with parchment paper. Combine flour and salt in small bowl.

2. For cookies, beat 1 cup butter and 1¼ cups granulated sugar in large bowl with electric mixer at medium speed until light and fluffy. Add egg yolk; beat until blended. Add sour cream; beat until well blended. Gradually add flour mixture at low speed until well blended.

3. Shape teaspoonfuls of dough into balls. Place on prepared cookie sheets; flatten slightly. Combine remaining 1 tablespoon granulated sugar, nutmeg and ginger in small bowl; sprinkle over cookies.

4. Bake 12 minutes or until edges are golden. Cool on cookie sheets 5 minutes. Remove to wire racks; cool completely.

5. For filling, beat ½ cup butter and shortening in medium bowl until well blended. Add powdered sugar and brandy; beat until well blended. Spread or pipe filling on flat side of half of cookies. Top with remaining cookies, flat side down.

FROSTED BUTTER COOKIES

Makes about 3 dozen cookies

COOKIES

1½ cups (3 sticks) butter, softened

¾ cup granulated sugar

3 egg yolks

2 tablespoons orange juice

1 teaspoon vanilla

3 cups all-purpose flour

1 teaspoon baking powder

½ teaspoon salt

FROSTING

4 cups powdered sugar

½ cup (1 stick) butter, softened

3 to 4 tablespoons milk

2 teaspoons vanilla

Food coloring

1. For cookies, beat 1½ cups butter and granulated sugar in large bowl with electric mixer at medium-high speed until creamy. Add egg yolks; beat until light and fluffy. Beat in orange juice and vanilla. Gradually add flour, baking powder and salt at low speed until well mixed. Wrap dough in plastic wrap; refrigerate 2 to 3 hours or until firm.

2. Preheat oven to 350°F. Roll out dough, half at a time, to ¼-inch thickness on floured surface. Cut dough with desired cookie cutters. Place 1 inch apart on ungreased cookie sheets. Bake 6 to 10 minutes or until edges are lightly browned. Remove to wire racks; cool completely.

3. For frosting, beat powdered sugar, ½ cup butter, milk and vanilla in bowl until fluffy. Divide frosting among small bowls and tint with food coloring. Frost cookies.

TIP: If desired, decorate cookies with Royal Icing (page 130 or 141) instead of, or in addition to, the buttercream frosting. To make cookie ornaments, poke a hole through the top of the cookies with a drinking straw before they bake. If the hole closes up during baking, poke it again with the straw while the cookies are still warm.

HOLIDAY BISCOTTI

Makes about 2 dozen biscotti

2⅓ cups all-purpose flour

1½ teaspoons baking powder

¾ cup sugar

½ cup (1 stick) butter, softened

2 eggs

1 teaspoon vanilla

1½ cups dried cranberries

1 cup shelled pistachio nuts (about 4¼ ounces)

1. Preheat oven to 375°F. Line cookie sheet with parchment paper. Combine flour and baking powder in medium bowl.

2. Beat sugar and butter in large bowl with electric mixer at medium speed until creamy. Beat in eggs and vanilla just until blended. Gradually add flour mixture, beating well at low speed after each addition. Stir in cranberries and pistachios.

3. Divide dough into thirds. Shape each piece into 9×2-inch log. (If dough is sticky, lightly dust hands with flour.) Place logs on prepared cookie sheet.

4. Bake 25 minutes or until tops are lightly browned (logs will be soft to the touch). Cool on cookie sheet until cool enough to handle. Cut logs diagonally into ½- to ¾-inch-thick slices using serrated knife.

5. *Reduce oven temperature to 325°F.* Place slices, cut side up, on cookie sheet (slices may touch). Bake 8 to 10 minutes or until edges are golden brown. Turn slices over; bake 8 to 10 minutes or until edges are golden brown. Remove to wire rack; cool completely. Store in airtight container.

CHOCOLATE REINDEER

Makes about 2 dozen cookies

1 cup granulated
   sugar

1 cup (2 sticks) butter,
   softened

1 egg

1 teaspoon vanilla

2 ounces semisweet
   chocolate, melted

2¼ cups all-purpose
   flour

1 teaspoon baking
   powder

¼ teaspoon salt

   Royal Icing (page
   130 or 141)

   Assorted sprinkles
   and decors

1. Beat granulated sugar and butter in large bowl with electric mixer at high speed until fluffy. Beat in egg and vanilla. Add melted chocolate; beat until well blended. Add flour, baking powder and salt; beat until well blended. Divide dough in half. Shape each half into disc. Wrap separately in plastic wrap; refrigerate 2 hours or until firm.

2. Preheat oven to 325°F. Grease cookie sheets. Roll out dough on well-floured surface to ¼-inch thickness. Cut out shapes with 4-inch reindeer-shaped cookie cutter. Place cutouts 2 inches apart on prepared cookie sheets. Refrigerate 10 minutes.

3. Bake 13 to 15 minutes or until set. Cool completely on cookie sheets.

4. Prepare Royal Icing. Pipe icing onto reindeer; decorate as desired.

RUM FRUITCAKE COOKIES

Makes about 6 dozen cookies

3   cups all-purpose
     flour

2   teaspoons baking
     powder

1   teaspoon baking
     soda

1   teaspoon salt

2   cups (8 ounces)
     chopped candied
     mixed fruit

1   cup nuts, coarsely
     chopped

1   cup raisins

1   cup sugar

¾   cup shortening

3   eggs

⅓   cup orange juice

1   tablespoon rum
     extract

1. Preheat oven to 375°F. Line cookie sheets with parchment paper. Combine flour, baking powder, baking soda and salt in medium bowl. Add candied fruit, nuts and raisins.

2. Beat sugar and shortening in large bowl with electric mixer at medium speed until fluffy. Add eggs, orange juice and rum extract; beat 2 minutes. Stir flour mixture into shortening mixture. Drop dough by rounded teaspoonfuls 2 inches apart onto prepared cookie sheets.

3. Bake 10 to 12 minutes or until golden brown. Cool on cookie sheets 2 minutes. Remove to wire racks; cool completely.

CANDY–STUDDED WREATHS

Makes about 2 dozen cookies

1 cup (2 sticks) butter, softened

½ cup powdered sugar

2 tablespoons packed brown sugar

¼ teaspoon salt

1 egg

1 teaspoon vanilla

2 cups all-purpose flour

4 to 5 drops green food coloring

Mini red and green candy-coated chocolate pieces

1. Beat butter, powdered sugar, brown sugar and salt in large bowl with electric mixer at medium speed 2 minutes or until light and fluffy. Add egg and vanilla; beat until well blended. Add flour, ½ cup at a time, beating well at low speed after each addition.

2. Divide dough in half; set one half aside. Add green color to remaining dough; beat until blended. Shape dough into discs. Wrap separately in plastic wrap; refrigerate 1 hour.

3. Preheat oven to 300°F. Shape green dough into 28 (5-inch) ropes. Repeat with plain dough. For each wreath, twist one green and one plain rope together, pressing ends together. Place on ungreased cookie sheets. Press candies onto wreaths.

4. Bake 15 to 18 minutes or until lightly browned. Cool on cookie sheets 5 minutes. Remove to wire racks; cool completely.

CHOCOLATE–DIPPED CINNAMON THINS

Makes about 2 dozen cookies

1¼ cups all-purpose flour

1½ teaspoons ground cinnamon

¼ teaspoon salt

1 cup (2 sticks) butter, softened

1 cup powdered sugar

1 egg

1 teaspoon vanilla

4 ounces bittersweet chocolate, melted

1. Combine flour, cinnamon and salt in small bowl. Beat butter in large bowl with electric mixer at medium speed until light and fluffy. Add powdered sugar; beat well. Add egg and vanilla. Gradually add flour mixture at low speed just until blended.

2. Place dough on sheet of waxed paper. Using waxed paper to hold dough, roll back and forth to form log about 2½ inches in diameter and 12 inches long. Wrap tightly in plastic wrap; refrigerate at least 2 hours or until firm. (Log may be frozen up to 3 months; thaw in refrigerator before baking.)

3. Preheat oven to 350°F. Cut dough into ¼-inch-thick slices. Place 2 inches apart on ungreased cookie sheets. Bake 10 minutes or until set. Cool on cookie sheets 2 minutes. Remove to wire racks; cool completely.

4. Dip each cookie into melted chocolate, coating 1 inch up sides. Transfer to wire racks or waxed paper; let stand at room temperature about 30 minutes or until chocolate is set. Store cookies between sheets of waxed paper at room temperature or in refrigerator.

SNOWPEOPLE COOKIES

Makes 1 dozen snowpeople

2¼ cups all-purpose flour

½ teaspoon baking soda

1 package (8 ounces) cream cheese, softened

1 cup powdered sugar

½ cup (1 stick) butter, softened

½ teaspoon almond extract

Additional sifted powdered sugar

12 sticks red or striped chewing gum

Mini candy-coated chocolate pieces

Red gummy candies, flattened and trimmed

Decorating icing

1. Preheat oven to 325°F. Line cookie sheets with parchment paper. Combine flour and baking soda in medium bowl.

2. Beat cream cheese, 1 cup powdered sugar, butter and almond extract in large bowl with electric mixer at medium speed until well blended.

3. Shape dough into equal number of ½-inch, 1-inch and 1½-inch diameter balls. Using one small, medium and large ball per snowperson, place balls, nearly touching, on prepared cookie sheets. Flatten each ball to ¼-inch thickness using bottom of glass dipped in flour.

4. Bake about 15 minutes or until edges are lightly browned. Cool on cookie sheets 1 minute. Remove to wire racks; cool completely.

5. Sprinkle each snowperson with additional sifted powdered sugar. Using one stick of gum, make scarf with fringed ends for each snowperson. Use chocolate pieces for eyes and gummy candies for mouths, securing with decorating icing.

BROWNED BUTTER SPRITZ COOKIES

Makes about 8 dozen cookies

1½ cups (3 sticks) butter

2½ cups all-purpose flour

¼ cup cake flour

¼ teaspoon salt

½ cup granulated sugar

¼ cup powdered sugar

1 egg yolk

1 teaspoon vanilla

⅛ teaspoon almond extract

1. Melt butter in medium heavy saucepan over medium heat until light amber, stirring frequently. Pour butter into large bowl. Cover and refrigerate 2 hours or until solid.

2. Preheat oven to 350°F. Let browned butter stand at room temperature 15 minutes. Combine all-purpose flour, cake flour and salt in small bowl.

3. Beat browned butter, granulated sugar and powdered sugar in large bowl with electric mixer at medium speed until light and fluffy. Add egg yolk, vanilla and almond extract; beat until well blended. Add flour mixture; beat until well blended.

4. Fit cookie press with desired plate. Fill press with dough; press dough 1 inch apart on ungreased cookie sheets. If desired, change plates for different shapes after each batch.

5. Bake 10 minutes or until lightly browned. Cool on cookie sheets 5 minutes. Remove to wire racks; cool completely.

TIP: To add even more holiday sparkle to these cookies, press red or green glacé cherry halves into the centers before baking, or sprinkle with decorating sugar. For trees or wreaths, tint the dough with green food coloring before pressing.

BUTTERY ALMOND CUTOUTS

Makes about 3 dozen cookies

1½ cups granulated sugar

1 cup (2 sticks) butter, softened

¾ cup sour cream

2 eggs

3 teaspoons almond extract, divided

1 teaspoon vanilla

4⅓ cups all-purpose flour

1 teaspoon baking powder

1 teaspoon baking soda

½ teaspoon salt

2 cups powdered sugar

2 tablespoons milk

1 tablespoon light corn syrup

Assorted food coloring, decorating gels, decorating sugars, sprinkles and decors

1. Beat granulated sugar and butter in large bowl with electric mixer at medium speed until light and fluffy. Add sour cream, eggs, 2 teaspoons almond extract and vanilla; beat until smooth. Add flour, baking powder, baking soda and salt; beat until well blended. Divide dough into four pieces; shape each piece into disc. Wrap each disc tightly with plastic wrap. Refrigerate at least 3 hours or up to 3 days.

2. For icing, combine powdered sugar, milk, corn syrup and remaining 1 teaspoon almond extract in small bowl; stir until smooth. Cover and refrigerate until ready to use or up to 3 days.

3. Preheat oven to 375°F. Roll out dough on floured surface to ¼-inch thickness. Cut out shapes using 2½-inch cookie cutters. Place cutouts 2 inches apart on ungreased cookie sheets. Bake 7 to 8 minutes or until edges are set and lightly browned. Remove to wire racks; cool completely.

4. Tint icing with desired food coloring. Frost and decorate cookies as desired; let stand until set.

NOTE: To freeze dough, place wrapped discs in resealable food storage bags. Thaw at room temperature before using. Or cut out dough, bake and cool cookies completely. Freeze unglazed cookies for up to 2 months. Thaw and glaze as desired.

HOLIDAY TRIPLE CHOCOLATE YULE LOGS

Makes about 3 dozen cookies

1¾ cups all-purpose flour

¾ cup powdered sugar

¼ cup unsweetened cocoa powder

⅛ teaspoon salt

1 cup (2 sticks) butter, softened

1 teaspoon vanilla

1 cup white chocolate chips

Chocolate sprinkles

1. Combine flour, powdered sugar, cocoa and salt in medium bowl. Beat butter and vanilla in large bowl with electric mixer at medium speed until fluffy. Gradually beat in flour mixture until well blended. Wrap dough in plastic wrap; refrigerate 30 minutes or until firm.

2. Preheat oven to 350°F. Shape dough into 2-inch logs about ½ inch thick. Place 2 inches apart on ungreased cookie sheets.

3. Bake 12 minutes or until set. Cool on cookie sheets 2 minutes. Remove to wire racks; cool completely.

4. Place white chocolate chips in small microwavable bowl. Microwave on HIGH 45 seconds; stir until completely melted. Place chocolate sprinkles in another small bowl. Dip both ends of cookies into melted white chocolate, then into chocolate sprinkles. Place on wire racks. Let stand 30 minutes or until set.

♥

SANTA'S FAVORITE COOKIES

GINGERBREAD PEOPLE

Makes about 4 dozen cookies

½ cup (1 stick) butter, softened

½ cup packed brown sugar

⅓ cup water

⅓ cup molasses

1 egg

4 cups all-purpose flour

2 teaspoons baking soda

1 teaspoon ground ginger

½ teaspoon ground allspice

½ teaspoon ground cinnamon

½ teaspoon ground cloves

Royal Icing (page 130 or 141)

Assorted candies

1. Beat butter and brown sugar in large bowl with electric mixer at medium speed until creamy. Add water, molasses and egg; beat until blended. Add flour, baking soda, ginger, allspice, cinnamon and cloves; beat until well blended. Shape dough into disc; wrap tightly with plastic wrap. Refrigerate 2 hours or until firm.

2. Preheat oven to 350°F. Line cookie sheets. with parchment paper. Roll out dough on lightly floured surface with lightly floured rolling pin to ⅛-inch thickness. Cut out shapes with cookie cutters. Place cutouts 2 inches apart on prepared cookie sheets.

3. Bake 12 to 15 minutes or until set. Cool on cookie sheets 1 minute. Remove to wire racks; cool completely.

4. Prepare Royal Icing. Decorate cookies with icing and candies. Store in airtight containers.

GIFTS FROM A JAR

MEMORABLE GIFT GIVING

Create an unforgettable gift for your friends and family by giving them a homemade gift jar filled with the ingredients to make delicious cookies, bars, breads, soups, snacks and more. Fill the jars as directed and add your own personal decorating touch. The results: a beautiful gift that will make a lasting impression. Since most of the ingredients are premeasured and in the jar, recipe preparation is quick and easy.

Keep the following tips in mind when preparing your gift jars.

• Always use a food-safe jar with an airtight lid.

• Make sure the jar is completely dry before filling it with ingredients.

• Use the jar size called for in the recipe.

• Measure each ingredient accurately.

• For ease in filling, use a canning funnel and a ¼-cup dry measuring cup.

• Combine dry ingredients like flour, baking soda and salt together in a bowl before adding them to the jar.

• Fill several jars at once for make-ahead gifts.

• After the jar is filled, make sure to replace the lid securely. Include the recipe and preparation instructions on a gift tag. Cover the top of the jar with a 9- or 10-inch circle of fabric, if desired. Tie the fabric and the gift tag onto the jar with raffia, ribbon, string, yarn or twine.

GIFTS FROM A JAR

SPICED SHORTBREAD COOKIE MIX

Makes one 1-quart jar

3 cups all-purpose flour	½ teaspoon ground ginger
½ teaspoon salt	¼ teaspoon grated nutmeg
½ teaspoon ground cinnamon	⅛ teaspoon ground cloves
	¾ cup sugar

1. Combine flour, salt, cinnamon, ginger, nutmeg and cloves in large bowl; mix well. Pour by cupfuls into 1-quart wide-mouth jar with tight-fitting lid; pack down well. Place sugar in small food storage bag. Force air from bag; close with twist tie and cut off excess. Place bag in jar; pack down firmly. Seal jar.

2. Cover top of jar with fabric. Attach recipe with raffia or ribbon.

SPICED SHORTBREAD COOKIES

Makes 3½ dozen cookies

1½ cups (3 sticks) unsalted butter, softened	1 jar Spiced Shortbread Cookie Mix

1. Beat butter in large bowl with electric mixer at medium speed 2 minutes or until smooth. Add sugar from bag; beat until blended. Add flour mixture from jar; mix on low speed just until blended. Press evenly into 13×9-inch baking pan dusted with flour; score into bars and pierce with fork. Cover and refrigerate at least 2 hours.

2. Preheat oven to 300°F. Line two baking sheets with parchment paper. Cut dough along score lines; place on prepared baking sheets.

3. Bake 20 to 30 minutes or until cookies are set, rotating pans once. Remove to wire rack; cool completely.

WHITE CHOCOLATE BIG COOKIE MIX

Makes one 1½-quart jar

2½ cups all-purpose flour	¾ cup packed brown sugar
1 teaspoon baking soda	¾ cup pecan halves, coarsely chopped
½ teaspoon salt	
⅔ cup unsweetened cocoa powder	½ cup golden raisins
1 cup granulated sugar	1 package (11 ounces) white chocolate chips

1. Combine flour, baking soda and salt in medium bowl; stir well. Transfer 1¼ cups flour mixture to another bowl. Stir ⅓ cup cocoa into remaining flour mixture.

2. Pour ¾ cup flour mixture into 1½-quart wide-mouth jar with tight-fitting lid; pack down well. Layer with ¾ cup cocoa mixture, remaining ⅓ cup cocoa, remaining flour mixture, remaining cocoa mixture, ½ cup granulated sugar, brown sugar and remaining ½ cup granulated sugar; pack down well after each layer. Add pecans, raisins and chocolate chips; pack down lightly after each layer. Seal jar.

3. Cover top of jar with fabric. Attach recipe to jar with raffia or ribbon.

WHITE CHOCOLATE BIG COOKIES

Makes about 2 dozen cookies

1½ cups (3 sticks) butter, softened

2 eggs

2 teaspoons vanilla

1 jar White Chocolate Big Cookie Mix

1. Preheat oven to 350°F. Line cookie sheets with parchment paper.

2. Beat butter in large bowl with electric mixer until smooth. Beat in eggs, one at a time. Beat in vanilla. (Mixture may appear curdled.) Pour contents of jar into another large bowl; mix well. Stir into butter mixture until well blended.

3. Drop dough by ¼ cupfuls 4 inches apart onto prepared cookie sheets; flatten slightly.

4. Bake 12 to 14 minutes or until firm in center. Cool on cookie sheets 5 minutes. Remove to wire rack; cool completely.

CHOCOLATE BUTTERSCOTCH BAR MIX

Makes one 1-quart jar

2¼ cups all-purpose flour	⅓ cup semisweet chocolate chips
2 teaspoons baking powder	
½ teaspoon salt	⅓ cup butterscotch chips
1½ cups packed brown sugar	¼ cup milk chocolate chips

1. Combine flour, baking powder and salt in medium bowl; mix well. Pour ¾ cup flour mixture into 1-quart wide-mouth jar with tight-fitting lid; pack down firmly. Add ½ cup brown sugar; pack down firmly. Repeat layers two more times; pack down firmly after each layer. Add chips; pack down firmly after each layer. Seal jar.

2. Cover top of jar with fabric. Attach recipe with raffia or ribbon.

CHOCOLATE BUTTERSCOTCH BARS

Makes 32 bars

1 cup (2 sticks) butter, softened	1 jar Chocolate Butterscotch Bar Mix
2 eggs	

1. Preheat oven to 350°F. Grease 15×10-inch jelly-roll pan.

2. Beat butter in large bowl with electric mixer at medium-high speed until light and fluffy. Add eggs; beat until well blended. Add contents of jar; stir just until blended. Spread batter evenly in prepared pan.

3. Bake 25 to 30 minutes or until edges are lightly browned and toothpick inserted into center comes out clean. Cool in pan 20 minutes. Cut into bars. Remove bars to wire rack; cool completely.

PISTACHIO SHORTBREAD CLUSTER MIX

Makes one 1-quart jar

1 cup shortbread cookie pieces

1 cup coarsely chopped salted pistachios

1½ cups white chocolate chips

½ cup diced dried pineapple* or golden raisins

Lightly coat knife with nonstick cooking spray before cutting to prevent sticking.

1. Place cookie pieces into 1-quart wide-mouth jar with tight-fitting lid. Add ½ cup pistachios, ¾ cup chocolate chips, pineapple, remaining pistachios and remaining chocolate chips; pack down lightly after each layer. Seal jar.

2. Cover top of jar with fabric. Attach recipe to jar with raffia or ribbon.

PISTACHIO SHORTBREAD CLUSTERS

Makes 4 dozen clusters

1 tablespoon shortening

1 jar Pistachio Shortbread Cluster Mix

1. Line baking sheet with parchment paper or waxed paper; set aside.

2. Place shortening in top of double boiler over simmering water. Add contents of jar. Stir frequently until shortening and white chocolate are melted and ingredients are evenly coated.

3. Drop mixture by heaping teaspoonfuls onto prepared baking sheet. Allow clusters to set until firm.

CHOCOLATE-PEANUT COOKIE MIX

Makes one 1-quart jar

2¼ cups all-purpose flour

1 teaspoon baking soda

¼ teaspoon salt

¾ cup packed brown sugar

¾ cup granulated sugar

2 cups chopped chocolate-covered peanuts

1. Combine flour, baking soda and salt in medium bowl; mix well. Pour into 1-quart jar with tight-fitting lid; pack down firmly. Layer with brown sugar, granulated sugar, and peanuts; pack down firmly after each layer. Seal jar.

2. Cover top of jar with fabric. Attach recipe to jar with raffia or ribbon.

CHOCOLATE-PEANUT COOKIES

Makes about 5 dozen cookies

1 cup (2 sticks) butter, softened

2 eggs

1 teaspoon vanilla

1 jar Chocolate-Peanut Cookie Mix

1. Preheat oven to 375°F.

2. Beat butter in large bowl with electric mixer at medium-high speed until smooth. Beat in eggs, one at a time, and vanilla. (Mixture may appear curdled.) Pour contents of jar into medium bowl; mix well. Stir into butter mixture until well blended.

3. Drop dough by rounded teaspoonfuls 2 inches apart onto cookie sheets.

4. Bake 9 to 11 minutes or until edges are lightly browned. Remove to wire racks; cool completely.

HOLIDAY CHOCOLATE RASPBERRY BAR MIX

Makes one 1-quart jar

1⅓ cups all-purpose flour

1 teaspoon baking powder

½ teaspoon salt

¼ teaspoon baking soda

⅓ cup unsweetened cocoa powder

1 cup packed brown sugar

⅔ cup red and green mini candy-coated chocolate pieces

1 cup old-fashioned oats

1. Combine flour, baking powder, salt and baking soda in medium bowl; stir well. Pour ⅔ cup flour mixture into 1-quart wide-mouth jar with tight-fitting lid; pack down well. Add cocoa, ½ cup brown sugar, remaining flour mixture and remaining brown sugar to jar; pack down well after each layer. Add candies and oats; pack down lightly after each layer. Seal jar.

2. Cover top of jar with fabric. Attach recipe to jar with raffia or ribbon.

HOLIDAY CHOCOLATE RASPBERRY BARS

Makes 16 bars

½ cup (1 stick) butter, softened

2 eggs

1 jar Holiday Chocolate Raspberry Bar Mix

⅓ cup seedless raspberry jam

1. Preheat oven to 350°F. Grease 9-inch square baking pan.

2. Beat butter in large bowl until smooth. Beat in eggs until blended. (Mixture may look curdled.) Add contents of jar; stir until well blended. Reserve 1 cup dough; spread remaining dough into prepared pan. Spread jam evenly over dough to within ½ inch of edges. Drop teaspoonfuls of reserved dough over jam.

3. Bake 25 to 30 minutes or until bars are slightly firm near edges. Cool completely in pan on wire rack. Cut into bars.

ULTIMATE WHITE AND DARK CHOCOLATE COOKIE MIX

Makes one 1½-quart jar

2⅓ cups all-purpose flour

1 teaspoon baking soda

¼ teaspoon salt

¾ cup granulated sugar

¾ cup packed brown sugar

1½ cups semisweet chocolate chips

1½ cups white chocolate chips

1 cup coarsely chopped pecans

1. Combine flour, baking soda and salt in medium bowl; mix well. Place granulated sugar, brown sugar, flour mixture, semisweet chocolate chips, white chocolate chips and pecans in 1½-quart wide-mouth jar; pack down well after each layer. Seal jar.

2. Cover top of jar with fabric. Attach recipe to jar with raffia or ribbon.

ULTIMATE WHITE AND DARK CHOCOLATE COOKIES

Makes about 6 dozen cookies

1 cup (2 sticks) butter, softened

2 eggs

2 tablespoons almond-flavored liqueur or water

1 teaspoon vanilla

1 jar Ultimate White and Dark Chocolate Cookie Mix

1. Preheat oven to 375°F.

2. Beat butter in large bowl with electric mixer until smooth. Beat in eggs, liqueur and vanilla. Pour contents of jar into medium bowl; mix well. Stir into butter mixture until well blended. Drop dough by teaspoonfuls 2 inches apart onto ungreased cookie sheets.

3. Bake 8 to 10 minutes or until edges are lightly browned. Remove to wire racks; cool completely.

A

Apple Butter Cookies with Penuche Frosting, 62

Apples
Apple Butter Cookies with Penuche Frosting, 62
Autumn Apple Bars, 58
Apricot Biscotti, 66
Argentinean Caramel-Filled Crescents (Pasteles), 122
Autumn Apple Bars, 58

B

Bacon: Caramel Bacon Nut Brownies, 100
Bar Cookies
Autumn Apple Bars, 58
Cherry Cheesecake Swirl Bars, 110
Chocolate Butterscotch Bars, 178
Chocolate Caramel Bars, 98
Dulce de Leche Blondies, 112
Hawaiian Bars, 106
Shortbread Turtle Cookie Bars, 114
Tangy Lemon Raspberry Bars, 104
Toffee Bars, 95
Basic Oatmeal Cookies, 10
Belgian Tuile Cookies, 128
Biscotti
Apricot Biscotti, 66
Hazelnut Biscotti, 138
Holiday Biscotti, 152
Black and White Hearts, 30
Black and White Sandwich Cookies, 72
Bolivian Almond Cookies (Alfajores de Almendras), 126
Browned Butter Spritz Cookies, 164
Brownies
Chewy Peanut Butter Brownies, 116
Chocolate Chip Sour Cream Brownies, 96

Brownies *(continued)*
Classic Brownies, 35
Cocoa-Orange-Cranberry Bars, 60
Fruit and Pecan Brownies, 108
Holiday Chocolate Raspberry Bars, 184
White Chocolate Peppermint Brownies, 102
Butter Pecan Crisps, 22
Butterscotch
Butterscotch-Coconut Oatmeal Cookies, 10
Chocolate Butterscotch Bars, 178
Triple Chipper Monsters, 12
Butterscotch-Coconut Oatmeal Cookies, 10
Buttery Almond Cutouts, 166
Buttery Lemongrass Wedges, 90

C

Cake Mix
Chinese Almond Cookies, 119
Chocolate Cherry Cookies, 68
Peanut Blossoms, 9
Candy-Studded Wreaths, 158
Caramel
Argentinean Caramel-Filled Crescents (Pasteles), 122
Caramel Bacon Nut Brownies, 100
Chocolate Caramel Bars, 98
Dulce de Leche Blondies, 112
Caramel Bacon Nut Brownies, 100
Cashew-Lemon Shortbread, 24
Cherries
Cherry Cheesecake Swirl Bars, 110
Chocolate Cherry Cookies, 68
Spumone Bars, 142

Cherry Cheesecake Swirl Bars, 110
Chewy Peanut Butter Brownies, 116
Chinese Almond Cookies, 119
Chippers
Chocolate Coconut Toffee Delights, 46
Classic Chocolate Chip Cookies, 20
Dark Chocolate Dreams, 42
Deep Dark Chocolate Drops, 50
Mocha Brownie Cookies, 40
Triple Chipper Monsters, 12
White Chocolate Macadamia Nut Cookies, 18
Chocolate Almond Meringue Sandwich Cookies, 88
Chocolate Butterscotch Bars, 178
Chocolate Caramel Bars, 98
Chocolate Cherry Cookies, 68
Chocolate Chip Sour Cream Brownies, 96
Chocolate Coconut Toffee Delights, 46
Chocolate-Dipped Cinnamon Thins, 160
Chocolate-Frosted Lebkuchen, 120
Chocolate Glaze, 36
Chocolate Hazelnut Sandwich Cookies, 84
Chocolate Marshmallow Drops, 36
Chocolate-Peanut Cookies, 182
Chocolate Raspberry Thumbprints, 64
Chocolate Reindeer, 154
Chocolate Strawberry Stackers, 78
Chocolate, 34–55
Belgian Tuile Cookies, 128
Black and White Hearts, 30
Black and White Sandwich Cookies, 72

Chocolate *(continued)*
Butter Pecan Crisps, 22
Caramel Bacon Nut
Brownies, 100
Chewy Peanut Butter
Brownies, 116
Chocolate Almond
Meringue Sandwich
Cookies, 88
Chocolate Butterscotch
Bars, 178
Chocolate Caramel Bars, 98
Chocolate Cherry Cookies,
68
Chocolate Chip Sour
Cream Brownies, 96
Chocolate-Dipped
Cinnamon Thins, 160
Chocolate-Frosted
Lebkuchen, 120
Chocolate Hazelnut
Sandwich Cookies, 84
Chocolate-Peanut Cookies,
182
Chocolate Raspberry
Thumbprints, 64
Chocolate Reindeer, 154
Chocolate Strawberry
Stackers, 78
Classic Chocolate Chip
Cookies, 20
Cocoa-Orange-Cranberry
Bars, 60
Flourless Peanut Butter
Cookies, 28
Fruit and Pecan Brownies,
108
Holiday Chocolate
Raspberry Bars, 184
Holiday Triple Chocolate
Yule Logs, 168
Peanut Blossoms, 9
Shortbread Turtle Cookie
Bars, 114
Toffee Bars, 95
Triple Chipper Monsters, 12
Ultimate White and Dark
Chocolate Cookies, 186
White Chocolate Big
Cookies, 176

Chunky Double Chocolate
Cookies, 48
Classic Brownies, 35
Classic Chocolate Chip
Cookies, 20
Cocoa-Orange-Cranberry
Bars, 60
Coconut
Argentinean Caramel-Filled
Crescents (Pasteles), 122
Butterscotch-Coconut
Oatmeal Cookies, 10
Chocolate Coconut Toffee
Delights, 46
Hawaiian Bars, 106
Coffee
Mocha Brownie Cookies, 40
Mocha Dots, 52
Cranberries
Ginger Polenta Cookies, 82
Holiday Biscotti, 152
Cutout Cookies
Black and White Hearts, 30
Buttery Almond Cutouts,
166
Chocolate Reindeer, 154
Festive Lebkuchen, 130
Finnish Spice Cookies
(Nissu Nassu), 140
Frosted Butter Cookies, 150
Gingerbread People, 170
Mini Lemon Sandwich
Cookies, 92
Tea Cookies, 71

D
Danish Cookie Rings
(Vanillekranser), 144
Dark Chocolate Dreams, 42
Deep Dark Chocolate Drops,
50
Drop Cookies
Apple Butter Cookies with
Penuche Frosting, 62
Basic Oatmeal Cookies, 10
Bolivian Almond Cookies
(Alfajores de Almendras),
126

Drop Cookies *(continued)*
Butterscotch-Coconut
Oatmeal Cookies, 10
Chocolate Coconut Toffee
Delights, 46
Chocolate-Frosted
Lebkuchen, 120
Chocolate-Peanut Cookies,
182
Chunky Double Chocolate
Cookies, 48
Classic Chocolate Chip
Cookies, 20
Dark Chocolate Dreams, 42
Deep Dark Chocolate
Drops, 50
Extra-Chocolatey Brownie
Cookies, 54
Hungarian Lemon Poppy
Seed Cookies, 134
Lemon Melts, 14
Malted Milk Cookies, 38
Mocha Brownie Cookies,
40
Pistachio Shortbread
Clusters, 181
Quebec Maple-Pecan
Drops, 124
Rum Fruitcake Cookies, 156
Triple Chipper Monsters, 12
Ultimate White and Dark
Chocolate Cookies, 186
White Chocolate Big
Cookies, 176
White Chocolate
Macadamia Nut Cookies,
18
Dulce de Leche Blondies, 112

E
Eggnog Sandwich Cookies,
148
Extra-Chocolatey Brownie
Cookies, 54

F
Festive Candy Canes, 147
Festive Lebkuchen, 130

Finnish Spice Cookies (Nissu Nassu), 140
Flourless Peanut Butter Cookies, 28
Frosted Butter Cookies, 150
Frostings and Glazes
 Penuche Frosting, 63
 Royal Icing, 130, 141
Fruit and Pecan Brownies, 108

G
Ginger
 Finnish Spice Cookies (Nissu Nassu), 140
 Gingerbread People, 170
 Ginger Polenta Cookies, 82
 New England Raisin Spice Cookies, 26
Gingerbread People, 170
Ginger Polenta Cookies, 82
Gooey Thumbprints, 57

H
Hawaiian Bars, 106
Hazelnut Biscotti, 138
Holiday Biscotti, 152
Holiday Chocolate Raspberry Bars, 184
Holiday Triple Chocolate Yule Logs, 168
Hungarian Lemon Poppy Seed Cookies, 134

L
Lemon
 Bolivian Almond Cookies (Alfajores de Almendras), 126
 Buttery Lemongrass Wedges, 90
 Cashew-Lemon Shortbread, 24
 Chocolate-Frosted Lebkuchen, 120
 Festive Lebkuchen, 130
 Hungarian Lemon Poppy Seed Cookies, 134
 Lemon Drops, 74
 Lemon Melts, 14

Lemon (continued)
 Mini Lemon Sandwich Cookies, 92
 Pebbernodders, 136
 Tangy Lemon Raspberry Bars, 104
Lemon Drops, 74
Lemon Melts, 14

M
Malted Milk Cookies, 38
Mini Lemon Sandwich Cookies, 92
Mocha Brownie Cookies, 40
Mocha Dots, 52

N
New England Raisin Spice Cookies, 26
Nuts
 Apple Butter Cookies with Penuche Frosting, 62
 Apricot Biscotti, 66
 Bolivian Almond Cookies (Alfajores de Almendras), 126
 Butter Pecan Crisps, 22
 Buttery Lemongrass Wedges, 90
 Caramel Bacon Nut Brownies, 100
 Cashew-Lemon Shortbread, 24
 Chinese Almond Cookies, 119
 Chocolate Almond Meringue Sandwich Cookies, 88
 Chocolate Caramel Bars, 98
 Chocolate-Frosted Lebkuchen, 120
 Chocolate Marshmallow Drops, 36
 Cocoa-Orange-Cranberry Bars, 60
 Danish Cookie Rings (Vanillekranser), 144
 Dark Chocolate Dreams, 42
 Extra-Chocolatey Brownie Cookies, 54

Nuts (continued)
 Fruit and Pecan Brownies, 108
 Ginger Polenta Cookies, 82
 Hawaiian Bars, 106
 Hazelnut Biscotti, 138
 Holiday Biscotti, 152
 Pistachio Shortbread Clusters, 181
 Quebec Maple-Pecan Drops, 124
 Rum Fruitcake Cookies, 156
 Shortbread Turtle Cookie Bars, 114
 Toffee Bars, 95
 White Chocolate Macadamia Nut Cookies, 18

O
Oats
 Basic Oatmeal Cookies, 10
 Butterscotch-Coconut Oatmeal Cookies, 10
 Quebec Maple-Pecan Drops, 124
 Shortbread Turtle Cookie Bars, 114
Old World Pfeffernüsse Cookies, 132
Orange
 Chocolate-Frosted Lebkuchen, 120
 Cocoa-Orange-Cranberry Bars, 60
 Rum Fruitcake Cookies, 156

P
Parmesan and Pine Nut Shortbread, 76
Peanut Blossoms, 9
Peanuts and Peanut Butter
 Chewy Peanut Butter Brownies, 116
 Chocolate-Peanut Cookies, 182
 Flourless Peanut Butter Cookies, 28
 Peanut Blossoms, 9

Pebbernodders, 136
Penuche Frosting, 63
Pistachio Shortbread Clusters, 181

Q
Quebec Maple-Pecan Drops, 124

R
Raisins: New England Raisin Spice Cookies, 26
Raspberry
Chocolate Raspberry Thumbprints, 64
Holiday Chocolate Raspberry Bars, 184
Tangy Lemon Raspberry Bars, 104
Refrigerator Cookies, 32
Rosemary Honey Shortbread Cookies, 86
Royal Icing, 130, 141
Rum Fruitcake Cookies, 156

S
Sandwich Cookies
Black and White Sandwich Cookies, 72
Chocolate Almond Meringue Sandwich Cookies, 88
Chocolate Hazelnut Sandwich Cookies, 84
Chocolate Strawberry Stackers, 78
Eggnog Sandwich Cookies, 148
Mini Lemon Sandwich Cookies, 92
Toffee Creme Sandwich Cookies, 80
Shaped Cookies
Candy-Studded Wreaths, 158
Cashew-Lemon Shortbread, 24
Chinese Almond Cookies, 119
Festive Candy Canes, 147

Shaped Cookies (continued)
Flourless Peanut Butter Cookies, 28
Holiday Triple Chocolate Yule Logs, 168
Lemon Drops, 74
New England Raisin Spice Cookies, 26
Old World Pfeffernüsse Cookies, 132
Peanut Blossoms, 9
Snickerdoodles, 16
Snowpeople Cookies, 162
Shortbread Turtle Cookie Bars, 114
Slice and Bake Cookies
Chocolate-Dipped Cinnamon Thins, 160
Chocolate Hazelnut Sandwich Cookies, 84
Chocolate Strawberry Stackers, 78
Ginger Polenta Cookies, 82
Parmesan and Pine Nut Shortbread, 76
Pebbernodders, 136
Refrigerator Cookies, 32
Rosemary Honey Shortbread Cookies, 86
Snickerdoodles, 16
Snowpeople Cookies, 162
Spiced Shortbread Cookies, 174
Spumone Bars, 142
Surprise Cookies, 44

T
Tangy Lemon Raspberry Bars, 104
Tea Cookies, 71
Thumbprint Cookies
Chocolate Cherry Cookies, 68
Chocolate Raspberry Thumbprints, 64
Gooey Thumbprints, 57
Mocha Dots, 52

Toffee
Chocolate Coconut Toffee Delights, 46
Toffee Bars, 95
Toffee Creme Sandwich Cookies, 80
Toffee Bars, 95
Toffee Creme Sandwich Cookies, 80
Triple Chipper Monsters, 12

U
Ultimate White and Dark Chocolate Cookies, 186

W
White Chocolate
Chunky Double Chocolate Cookies, 48
Cocoa-Orange-Cranberry Bars, 60
Dark Chocolate Dreams, 42
Holiday Triple Chocolate Yule Logs, 168
Pistachio Shortbread Clusters, 181
Shortbread Turtle Cookie Bars, 114
Triple Chipper Monsters, 12
Ultimate White and Dark Chocolate Cookies, 186
White Chocolate Big Cookies, 176
White Chocolate Macadamia Nut Cookies, 18
White Chocolate Peppermint Brownies, 102
White Chocolate Big Cookies, 176
White Chocolate Macadamia Nut Cookies, 18
White Chocolate Peppermint Brownies, 102

METRIC CONVERSION CHART

VOLUME MEASUREMENTS (dry)

1/8 teaspoon = 0.5 mL
1/4 teaspoon = 1 mL
1/2 teaspoon = 2 mL
3/4 teaspoon = 4 mL
1 teaspoon = 5 mL
1 tablespoon = 15 mL
2 tablespoons = 30 mL
1/4 cup = 60 mL
1/3 cup = 75 mL
1/2 cup = 125 mL
2/3 cup = 150 mL
3/4 cup = 175 mL
1 cup = 250 mL
2 cups = 1 pint = 500 mL
3 cups = 750 mL
4 cups = 1 quart = 1 L

VOLUME MEASUREMENTS (fluid)

1 fluid ounce (2 tablespoons) = 30 mL
4 fluid ounces (1/2 cup) = 125 mL
8 fluid ounces (1 cup) = 250 mL
12 fluid ounces (1 1/2 cups) = 375 mL
16 fluid ounces (2 cups) = 500 mL

WEIGHTS (mass)

1/2 ounce = 15 g
1 ounce = 30 g
3 ounces = 90 g
4 ounces = 120 g
8 ounces = 225 g
10 ounces = 285 g
12 ounces = 360 g
16 ounces = 1 pound = 450 g

DIMENSIONS

1/16 inch = 2 mm
1/8 inch = 3 mm
1/4 inch = 6 mm
1/2 inch = 1.5 cm
3/4 inch = 2 cm
1 inch = 2.5 cm

OVEN TEMPERATURES

250°F = 120°C
275°F = 140°C
300°F = 150°C
325°F = 160°C
350°F = 180°C
375°F = 190°C
400°F = 200°C
425°F = 220°C
450°F = 230°C

BAKING PAN SIZES

Utensil	Size in Inches/Quarts	Metric Volume	Size in Centimeters
Baking or Cake Pan (square or rectangular)	8×8×2	2 L	20×20×5
	9×9×2	2.5 L	23×23×5
	12×8×2	3 L	30×20×5
	13×9×2	3.5 L	33×23×5
Loaf Pan	8×4×3	1.5 L	20×10×7
	9×5×3	2 L	23×13×7
Round Layer Cake Pan	8×1½	1.2 L	20×4
	9×1½	1.5 L	23×4
Pie Plate	8×1¼	750 mL	20×3
	9×1¼	1 L	23×3
Baking Dish or Casserole	1 quart	1 L	—
	1½ quart	1.5 L	—
	2 quart	2 L	—

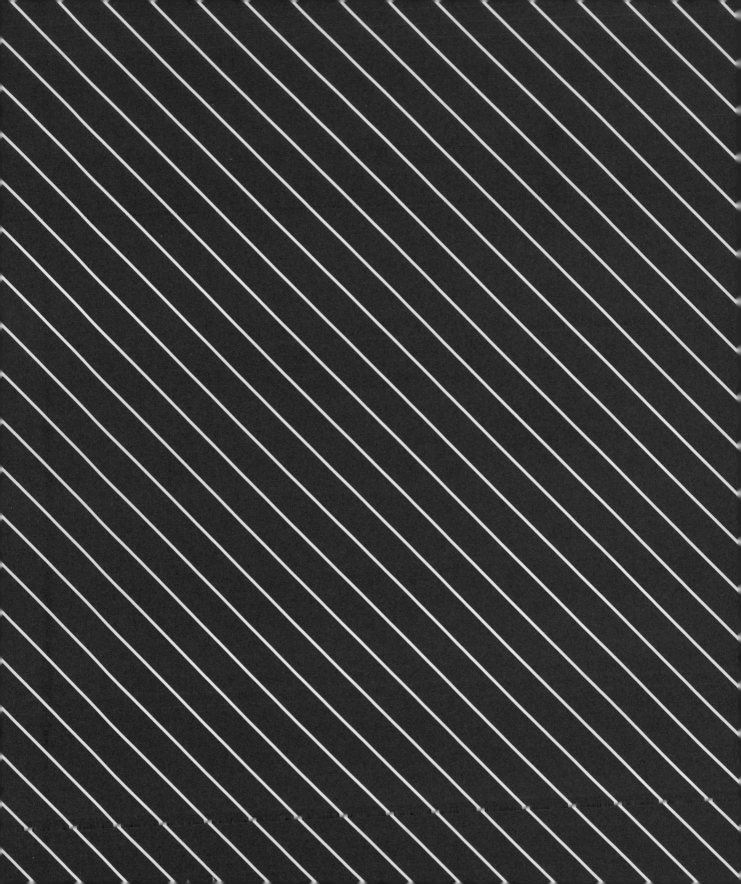